# SHORT WAI

## ——PUBS N

# *Bristol anu Bath*

Nigel Vile

COUNTRYSIDE BOOKS
NEWBURY, BERKSHIRE

.

Designed by Mon Mohan
Cover illustration by Colin Doggett
Photographs and maps by the author

Produced through MRM Associates Ltd., Reading
Typeset by Paragon Typesetters, Newton-le-Willows, Merseyside
Printed by J.W. Arrowsmith Ltd., Bristol

# Contents

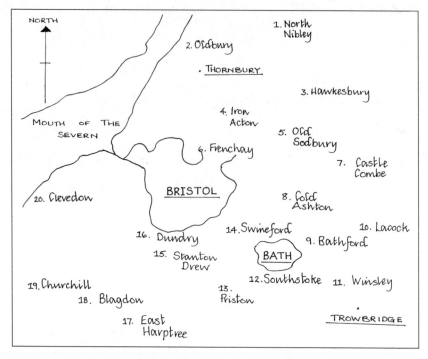

Area map showing the locations of the walks.

**Publisher's Note**

We hope that you obtain considerable enjoyment from this book; great care has been taken in its preparation. However, changes of landlord and actual closures are sadly not uncommon. Likewise, although at the time of publication all routes followed public rights of way or permitted paths, diversion orders can be made and permissions withdrawn.

We cannot of course be held responsible for such diversion orders and any inaccuracies in the text which result from these or any other changes to the routes nor any damage which might result from walkers trespassing on private property. We are anxious though that all details covering the walks and the pubs are kept up to date and would therefore welcome information from readers which would be relevant to future editions.

# Introduction

Bath and Bristol are renowned as two of the finest cities in the country. What is less well known is the rich variety of landscape that exists within just 20 miles of these historic settlements. To the west lie the Severn Estuary and the Bristol Channel, a unique environment of mud flats and estuarine wildlife. Northwards are the Cotswold Hills, a landscape of secluded valleys and stone villages. To the south of Bath and Bristol lie the Mendip Hills, a vast area of limestone upland, dissected and riddled by gorges and pot-holes. Finally, there is the common thread that links these two great cities – the river Avon. The river bank provides some of the most popular walking in the area.

Each of the walks in this volume is centred upon one of the many inns that grace the area around Bath and Bristol. Alongside the traditional freehouses and pubs owned by smaller independent breweries, are inns that belong to the large multinational conglomerates. In some instances, fine old inns were omitted simply because no suitable walk existed in the vicinity. On other occasions, an outstanding walk meant that the choice of pub was somewhat limited.

For each pub, a pen portrait has been included. This covers its history, its character, the food available and the range of beers and ales on offer. Clearly, the information is only accurate at a point in time, but it is more than adequate to give the reader an overall feel and impression of the pub.

Most pubs will be open at lunchtimes between 11.30 am and 2.30 pm, with food being served between 12 noon and 2 pm. Equally, in the evenings you can expect the opening hours to extend from 6 pm until 10.30 pm, with food available from around 7 pm. However, pub opening hours are the subject of constant change and variation, depending upon demand, seasonal factors and occasionally the whim of the landlord. Therefore, rather than specify opening hours in each case, only to be proven wrong by the time the book goes to print, each pub's telephone number is included should you wish to make a precise enquiry. Most pubs display their opening hours at their main entrance, enabling this information to be obtained before you set off on your walk.

The walks have been kept deliberately short, making them suitable for a broad range of walkers. Family groups, more mature persons or anyone simply wanting a pleasant hour or two of exercise will find plenty of ideas in the book to suit their needs. Clearly, walkers seeking a hike of Wainwright or Poucher proportions should look elsewhere! The various walks will provide a morning or an afternoon of exercise and interest, which can be followed by a relaxing meal and drink in the relevant pub.

Whilst the directions and sketch maps in the book are more than adequate for route-finding – compasses won't be necessary in this part of the world – I would always recommend that you carry the relevant OS map whilst out walking. The appropriate Landranger sheet has been specified in each case, and should be as much a part of your equipment as the obligatory waterproof clothing and stout footwear.

Parking should be done with due consideration. If you intend to visit the pub following the walk, then it is only common courtesy to seek the landlord's permission prior to using his car park at ten o'clock in the morning. On most occasions, landlords are only too happy to oblige. If you are doing one of the walks but not visiting the pub, then you have no right to use the patrons' car park. Whatever the circumstances, in every case I have indicated alternative parking arrangements in the vicinity of each pub.

At the end of your walk, you could well be hot and sticky, damp and muddy. It is only polite therefore to both the landlord and his other customers if you attempt some form of wash and brush-up after your walk. If nothing else, at least leave muddy walking boots in your car. Failure to follow these common courtesies has in the past made walkers unwelcome at one or two hostelries. I can understand the landlord's thinking!

Finally, I hope that this book will bring you many hours of pleasure. Not only do these walks open up the countryside around two of Britain's greatest cities, they also introduce some of our finest inns and public houses to a wider audience. I wish you many happy hours of walking.

Nigel A. Vile
Spring 1996

# 1 North Nibley
## The Black Horse Inn

The small village of North Nibley clings to the hillside below the Cotswold Edge, just a mile or two north of Wotton-under-Edge. Towering over the village is the Tyndale Monument, commemorating the 16th-century priest William Tyndale who first translated the New Testament into English. The Black Horse is one of the oldest buildings in the village that lays claim to being Tyndale's birthplace. Originally a coaching inn on the route between Wotton and Berkeley, the Black Horse is today a straightforward village pub, which offers a friendly welcome and a warm atmosphere to both locals and visitors alike.

The Black Horse is constructed of the local Cotswold stone, although much of the external stonework is now lost beneath a covering of whitewash. Internally, the inn consists of a long bar area with dining areas at either end. With its low, timbered ceilings and log fires, the inn will provide a relaxing atmosphere at the end of a walk on the nearby hillsides. In summer your food and drink can be enjoyed in the beer garden which lies behind the pub.

As well as restaurant-style meals, a full range of bar food is available at the Black Horse. The choices include ploughman's lunches, jacket potatoes, sandwiches and home-made soup, together with more substantial offerings such as beef, mushroom and Guinness pie, Madras beef curry, vegetable Mexicana and lamb goulash. The desserts are equally appealing, and include hot chocolate fudge cake and delicious treacle sponge pudding.

A number of Whitbread-related beers are available at the Black Horse. These include Boddingtons Bitter and Flowers Original. A beer from the nearby Wickwar Brewing Company is usually available, too. This might be the ever popular Brand Oak Bitter or the less common Cooper's WPA. Fine beers in an excellent Cotswold pub situated amidst a quite exceptional landscape.

Telephone: 01453 546841.

*How to get there:* North Nibley lies on the B4060 Cam road, just 2 miles north of Wotton-under-Edge. The Black Horse lies alongside a minor crossroads in the middle of the village.

*Parking:* There is a car park for patrons opposite the Black Horse, as well as roadside parking immediately in front of the inn.

*Length of the walk:* 3 miles. Map: OS Landranger 162 Gloucester and the Forest of Dean (inn GR 741958).

*Some of the best walking country in the Cotswolds lies in the immediate vicinity of North Nibley, a small village deep in the South Gloucestershire countryside. Secluded valleys and steep hillsides plunge down to the Severn Vale, with picturesque place-names such as Waterley Bottom and Millend giving a real flavour of the landscape. High on Nibley Knoll, towering above the village, is the Tyndale Monument. From the monument, visitors can obtain a quite exceptional view across the Severn Vale to the Forest of Dean and the distant Welsh Hills. An excellent walk which explores this hill country deep in the Southwolds.*

**The Walk**
Cross the B4060 alongside the Black Horse, and follow the lane opposite – The Street – for 300 yards to a small triangular green on the right. Turn right, and follow the signposted Cotswold Way out of North Nibley. At first the Way is a tarmac lane serving a few isolated

9

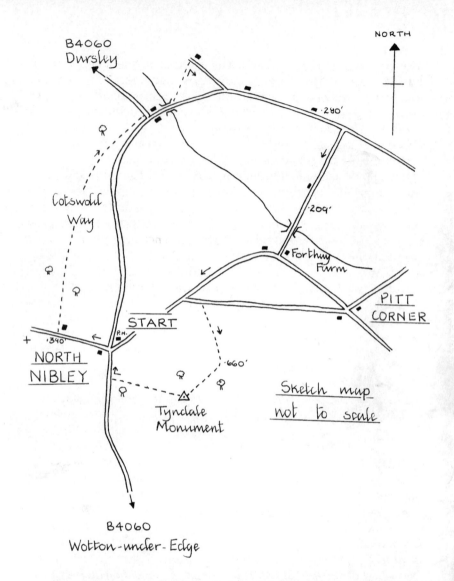

NORTH

B4060
Dursley

·280'

Cotswold
Way

·209'

● Forthay
Farm

PITT
CORNER

START

·340'

NORTH
NIBLEY

·660'

Tyndale
Monument

Sketch map
not to scale

B4060
Wotton-under-Edge

cottages, but it very quickly becomes a delightfully secluded green lane. In ½ mile, the path brings you again to the B4060.

Cross the main road with care – there are bends on either side – and follow the lane opposite signposted to Millend and Waterley Bottom. In 100 yards, just past a stone and brick cottage on the right, turn left off the lane to continue along the Cotswold Way as it enters an open field. At first, the Way climbs a steep bank up into the field before bearing half-left to cross to a stile in the opposite field boundary. In the next field, the Cotswold Way continues across to a stile and a secluded lane beside a detached house. The views behind on this leg of the walk are exceptional, with the village of North Nibley tucked in beneath the Cotswold Edge, overlooked by the Tyndale Monument.

Turn right along the lane, and follow this quiet byway for ½ mile until you come to the second right turn. Follow this unsigned turning, which rapidly descends into a small valley before climbing the opposite hillside to a junction alongside Forthay Farm. Turn right at this junction, along the lane signposted to North Nibley, and follow this quiet byway for 500 yards to the next road junction. Turn left, along the lane signposted to Waterley Bottom. In 100 yards, immediately before a residence called the Gables, cross a stile on the right of the road to follow a signposted footpath.

Follow the left-hand field boundary beyond this stile up the hillside onto the high wolds. The climb brings you into woodland, where you keep following the main path as it climbs steeply before reaching a stile at the top of the hill. Cross over a track into an old quarry where almost immediately you turn right onto a minor side path. This path climbs to reach a stile on the top edge of the quarry. Cross the pasture beyond this stile to reach the Tyndale Monument.

The view across the Severn Vale is quite special, so much so that a topograph marks the spot. You can assess the visibility from the landmarks you can see. On a good day, the Sugar Loaf Mountain (33 miles) should be visible. The Severn Bridge is shown as being 12 miles away, whilst nearer to hand is the village of Kingswood (2 miles). Just to the right of the monument, down the slope, a stile gives access into an area of woodland. Follow the steep, stepped path down through the woods for 200 yards to a junction. Turn left along a track which leads back to the B4060. At the main road, turn right and you will soon be back in the centre of North Nibley beside the Black Horse.

# ② Oldbury on Severn
## The Anchor Inn

Prior to extensive drainage schemes in the 17th and 18th centuries, Oldbury would literally have been in the Severn following high tides. Today the river is nearly 1 mile away, with the former flooded marshland now supporting rich pasture and the occasional cider apple orchard. The Anchor, with its inn sign displaying a mermaid, speaks of the seafaring traditions of this corner of the Severn Vale. In years gone by, coastal vessels would have sailed into Oldbury carrying coal from the Forest of Dean. The return cargo may well have been barrels of the local Kingston Black cider.

The Anchor, sitting alongside a small stream, is in fact a converted 16th-century mill. The inn is fashioned from the local pennant sandstone, and looks most delightful when the window boxes and creepers are in full flower. Internally, there is a beamed lounge and dining area. With high-backed settles, winged chairs and cushioned window seats, the Anchor's furnishings certainly match the inn's sense of history. In winter, a welcoming log fire will soon warm you up following a breezy walk along the Severn, whilst in summer you can enjoy a relaxing pint in the inn's garden.

The Anchor has earned a fine reputation for its food. The menu changes frequently, meaning that you will always find something new to enjoy no matter how often you visit the inn. Leek and potato bake, chicken and pineapple curry, boozy beef pie, filled Yorkshire puddings, local sausages … these are just a few examples of the many delicious dishes that may be available. If that is not enough, perhaps traditional apple crumble or even sticky toffee pudding will replace those calories lost on the walk.

With an entry in CAMRA's *Good Beer Guide*, serious drinkers will equally enjoy their visit to the Anchor. Whether it be a glass of Draught Bass, Butcombe Bitter, Marston's Pedigree or Theakston's Old Peculier, the thirst worked up on the walk will soon be well satisfied.

Telephone: 01454 413331.

*How to get there:* Follow the A38 northwards out of Bristol until, 2 miles beyond the B4061 Thornbury turning, Oldbury on Severn is signposted. Follow the well-marked route to the centre of the village, where you will find the Anchor.

*Yachts at Oldbury Pill.*

13

*Parking:* There is a car park for patrons opposite the Anchor, as well as room for careful roadside parking in the vicinity of the inn.

*Length of the walk:* 2½ miles. Map: OS Landranger 172 Bristol and Bath (inn GR 609923).

*From the Anchor, a gentle climb brings you to St Arilda's church. The location of the church atop a small knoll gives extensive views across the Severn to the Welsh Hills and the Forest of Dean. A quiet byway is followed down to the Severn, whose mighty waters lead you back into Oldbury. This is serious bird-watching country, with the mud flats revealed at low tide supporting any number of waders. Come armed with your field glasses and a bird-spotting guide, and you will soon understand what makes a twitcher tick! Dunlin, curlew and redshank are but three of the species to keep a lookout for.*

**The Walk**

Turn left outside the Anchor and, in just a few yards, right into Westmarsh Lane. In ¼ mile, immediately before Westmarsh House, cross a stile on the left into an adjoining field. Follow the right-hand field boundary uphill towards St Arilda's church. Beyond a stile in the top corner of the field, cross a small enclosure to reach the Oldbury to Thornbury road. A detour up to the church is almost obligatory to enjoy the extensive views across the Severn Vale. With its prominent hilltop location, it is not difficult to see why the church tower was for many years whitewashed to act as a landmark for river-borne traffic.

Turn right at the road and, in ¼ mile, right along a No Through Road. This is on the edge of the diminutive hamlet of Cowhill, where a local cider is produced using traditional methods. The press lies just along the through road on the right-hand side. Continue down the cul-de-sac lane to Lower Farm, beyond which the right-of-way becomes an unmetalled bridlepath. Where this path ends at a gateway, cross one open field to reach the banks of the Severn.

Follow the flood defences to the right in the direction of Oldbury Power Station. This is magnificent walking, with the waters of the Severn immediately to hand, and extensive views in all directions. All too soon, the path bears right along Oldbury Pill, home of the

14

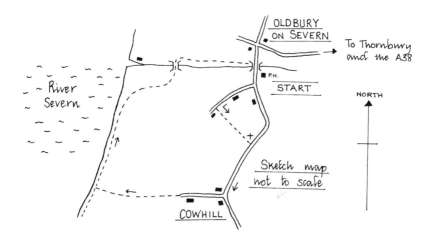

local sailing club. Cross the sluice across the pill, before turning right to follow the sailing club access lane down to Oldbury village and the Anchor. This short section of road walking can be avoided by following the grassy area alongside the pill.

# ③ Hawkesbury Upton
## The Beaufort Arms

Hawkesbury Upton is a hilltop village lying above the Cotswold Edge and the Severn Vale. Just a few miles to the east is the Badminton estate, not only home to the annual horse trials but also the ancestral home of the Beaufort family. It should come as no surprise, therefore, to find his lordship's portrait adorning the sign outside this village inn, especially in view of the fact that the Beaufort Arms was originally an 18th-century farmhouse on the Duke's estate. The inn is constructed of the local Cotswold stone, although much of the original stonework is now lost beneath a covering of whitewash and plaster. With barrels containing floral displays at the front, and a garden to the rear, the Beaufort Arms presents a handsome exterior to visitors.

Internally, the inn consists of public and lounge bars together with the blue and buff restaurant. A real country-feel exists throughout the Beaufort Arms, with its stone walls, open fireplaces, beams and animal prints. Various artefacts are displayed in the bars, including traditional yokes, a number of cider pots and a tin tray advertising Cotswold Beers brewed by the

Stroud Brewery.

The bar meals include ploughman's lunches, sandwiches, jacket potatoes and a range of snacks. These cover such choices as veggie burgers, cheeseburgers, ham, egg and chips and garlic bread. The restaurant menu is more extensive, and covers starters, grills, fish dishes, poultry, vegetarian meals, salads and desserts. For starters, customers might be tempted by the seafood cocktail. This could be followed by perhaps Scottish rainbow trout almondine or roast duck with black cherry sauce. Vegetarians might prefer the vegetable pancake with Provençal sauce. Finally, jam roly poly pudding or spotted dick would certainly restore those calories burnt off on the walk!

To accompany your meal, the Beaufort Arms offers an interesting range of beers. These might include Charles Wells Bombardier from Bedford, Wadworth 6X from Devizes or Brand Oak Bitter from the nearby village of Wickwar.

Telephone: 01454 23817.

*How to get there:* Hawkesbury Upton lies 1 mile west of the A46 Bath to Stroud road, 4 miles north of Old Sodbury. From Old Sodbury, head northwards until you reach the Petty France Hotel at Dunkirk. Shortly after the hotel, a left turn is signposted to Hawkesbury Upton. The Beaufort Arms is on the left-hand side in the middle of the village, facing the main street.

*Parking:* There is a car park for patrons at the Beaufort Arms, as well as room for roadside parking in the immediate vicinity of the inn. Just west of the inn is the village hall with its own large car park.

*Length of the walk:* 3½ miles. Map: OS Landranger 172 Bristol and Bath (inn GR 777870).

*Hawkesbury Upton lies high on the Cotswold Plateau. It is a large village best known for the Somerset Monument, a superb vantage point across the Severn Vale. The monument was erected in 1846 in memory of General Robert Edward Henry Somerset, a member of the Beaufort family. From the Somerset Monument, our steps follow the Cotswold Way through Frith Wood and Claypit Wood down to the Kilcott Valley. In early springtime, the woods are awash with*

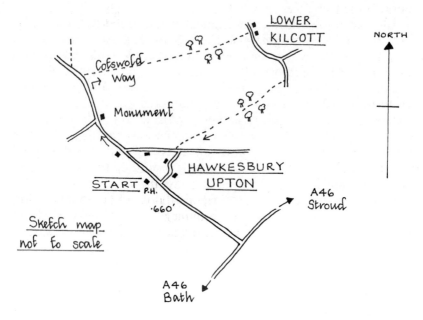

traditional English flora, making this a particularly worthwhile seasonal excursion. *From the delightfully secluded Kilcott Valley, a gentle climb through Small Coombe and Upton Coombe returns us to Hawkesbury Upton. A beautiful walk through the secluded Southwolds, that is all the better for being off the recognised tourist trail.*

**The Walk**
Turn left outside the Beaufort Arms, and follow the main street out of Hawkesbury Upton for ½ mile until you pass the Somerset Monument. Continue along the Hillesley road for another 400 yards (warning – no pavement) to a point where the road bears left and a prominent track continues directly ahead towards Splatt's Barn. At this point, turn right onto the signposted Cotswold Way. A short section of enclosed track leads to a gateway, beyond which you follow a well worn track to the far left-hand corner of a large field, a distance of some 600 yards.

In the corner of this field, the Way enters Frith Wood and immediately forks. The blue-arrowed path to the left is a bridlepath through the woods – we follow the yellow-arrowed footpath to the

18

right. This path follows a well defined route through the woods for ½ mile, before emerging into an open hilltop field above Long Coombe. Turn right, and follow the top edge of this field beside Frith Wood to the far corner, where a track is joined that is followed downhill to the Kilcott Valley. This is the archetypal Cotswold landscape – hillside sheep pasture and a valley bottom whose waters powered the occasional mill.

Turn right at the road in the valley bottom, keep right at the junction in just 400 yards, and in another 400 yards cross a stile on the right to follow a signposted footpath. Continue along this path through the delightful Small Coombe for ½ mile until, in a clearing, you reach a junction. Bear left, and follow the wooded valley to a gateway some 300 yards distant. Beyond this gateway, continue out of the woods beside a small stream, aiming for a gateway in the top left-hand corner of this first field. Beyond this gateway, continue along a well worn path that climbs gently out of the valley, crossing three fields before reaching a stile. Cross this stile, and follow a short section of enclosed track to a quiet lane. Follow the turning immediately opposite into Hawkesbury Upton. In the village, a right turn at the main street will soon return you to the Beaufort Arms.

# 4 Iron Acton
## The Lamb Inn

Since being bypassed by the B4058, Iron Acton – literally 'the oak settlement with iron mines' – has slipped into a period of gentle tranquillity. With the many period houses lining the High Street, it is clear why the village has become rather popular with commuters working in the heart of Bristol. At the eastern end of the High Street lies one of the older buildings in the village, the Lamb Inn dating from the 16th century. This substantial detached hostelry, with its attractive gabled windows, is constructed of the local pennant sandstone — albeit lost under a coating of whitewashed plaster. The history of the Lamb shows that William of Orange and Mary stayed under its roof in 1690, on their way to London.

This sense of history is evident as soon as you enter the inn. Darkwood beams are everywhere, along with exposed stonework, all carefully restored and preserved in pristine condition. With its prints – including illustrations of both the Lamb and the local manor – stone fireplaces, wooden settles and brasses, the inn enjoys a very traditional atmosphere.

A wide-ranging menu is available at the Lamb, with choices

covering chicken, fish and pasta dishes, ploughman's lunches, sandwiches, children's dishes and desserts. There is also an interesting item called 'Yvonne's Pie', a daily special named after the landlord's wife. On a recent visit, the filling of the day was cauliflower and cheese. A board in the bar displays the day's specials, which might typically include balti and naan, chicken, cheese and broccoli pie, chicken in a mushroom, onion and cream sauce or a trio of pasta. Pasta dishes, incidentally, are a strength of the Lamb's menu. If your main course still leaves a gap to fill, the desserts include such calorific extravaganzas as knickerbocker glory, fruit pies, banana split and hot chocolate fudge cake.

A good range of beers and ales is available at the Lamb. These might include various Whitbread brews, Flowers Original and Brand Oak Bitter from the nearby Wickwar Brewery. Alongside the Lamb is a good, shady garden, just the spot to enjoy a refreshing pint following a stroll along the Frome Valley Walkway south of Iron Acton.

Telephone: 01454 228265.

*How to get there:* Iron Acton lies on the B4058 midway between Bristol and Wotton-under-Edge. Leave the main road, which by-passes the village, and drive to the eastern end of the High Street, where you cannot miss the Lamb.

*Parking:* There is a car park for patrons of the Lamb, as well as extensive roadside parking in the immediate vicinity of the inn.

*Length of the walk:* 2½ miles. Map: OS Landranger 172 Bristol and Bath (inn GR 681836).

*This walk provides the opportunity to explore the historic village of Iron Acton, together, with the river Frome as it passes through the neighbouring countryside. Along the way, features of interest include the parish church, Algars Manor and Chill Wood. This deciduous woodland was formerly the site of iron workings, perhaps even lending its name to the village of Iron Acton. The manor enjoys a pleasant location alongside a small bridge over the Frome. Originally Tudor, the present house dates mainly from the 18th century. The whole area is a delightful rural oasis, sandwiched between various urban developments.*

*Monument at Iron Acton churchyard.*

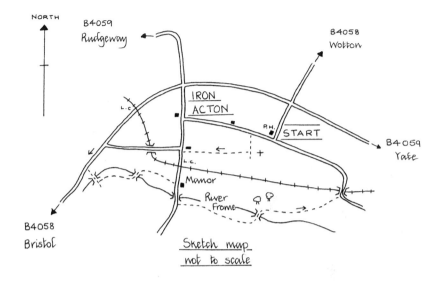

Sketch map
not to scale

## The Walk

Follow the High Street as far as Iron Acton church, where you turn left to follow a signposted footpath into the churchyard. Just past the church, turn right onto a path that tunnels beneath a neighbouring garden before reaching a stile. Follow the field boundary beyond this stile to a second stile and the village football pitch. Cross the pitch to reach a stile opposite – game permitting! – beyond which an enclosed path is followed for 200 yards to a road junction. Follow the road opposite, which crosses the mineral railway running from Yate to Thornbury before reaching the B4058.

Turn left at the main road, and follow the wide grass verge for 300 yards until you reach a bridlepath on the left signposted to Frampton End. Follow this path for 50 yards until it crosses the river Frome, before crossing a stile on the left to follow the Frome Valley Walkway. The path follows the river to the corner of the first field, beyond which an enclosed section of path runs the short distance to a bridge across the Frome. This bridge once carried a mineral railway from iron workings at Frampton through to Iron Acton. Cross the river, and continue following the Frome Valley Walkway through to Frampton End Road. As you approach this lane, the Walkway bears left away from the river to reach a stile besides the road.

Turn right and follow the lane down past Algars Manor and across the Frome, before turning left along the Walkway to continue along the riverbank. In 300 yards, you reach a sluice with Chill Wood across the river. It is worth making a brief detour to explore this former site of iron and coal workings. The walk itself continues following the south bank of the Frome until you reach a footbridge in just 150 yards. Cross this bridge, and follow the opposite bank of the river across the next two fields until you reach a stile. In the next field, cross to the far left-hand corner, walking away from the river.

In the far corner of this field you will find a grassy track, which is followed for 200 yards up to Nibley Lane. Turn left, and follow this lane over the Thornbury railway line and on for just under ½ mile back into Iron Acton. You reach a junction with the High Street, where a right turn will bring you back to the Lamb.

# Old Sodbury
## The Dog Inn

The inn sign outside the Dog will almost certainly catch your eye –
it is not every day that a sign carries a piece of verse. This one reads:

> This gate hangs well
> And hinders none
> Now up the hill before pass
> Step in and take a cheerful glass

With a welcome like this, who could resist passing through what
one guidebook describes as an 'interesting Tudor doorway' to see
what delights the Dog has to offer. Visitors will not be disappointed.
Although not enjoying the best of locations on a busy main road,
once inside the Dog a very traditional atmosphere awaits
customers. A long bar area, exposed stonework, beams, open
fireplaces, low ceilings and wall benches give the inn a relaxing air.

The Dog has earned a far-ranging reputation for its extensive
range of food. The menu covers upwards of 100 dishes, so allow
plenty of time to make your choices. Fish is a speciality, with red

mullet, squid, fresh sole and mussels being but a selection of the available dishes. Vegetarians are well catered for with options such as vegetarian moussaka and hazelnut and brown rice roast, whilst more traditional palates might prefer a steak and kidney pie or a portion of cottage pie. The children's menu is described as 'Puppy Food', and includes such favourites as burgers, chicken nuggets and fish fingers. The Dog also offers a wide selection of sweets, that extends from the traditional spotted dick with custard through to pear belle hélène and chocolate au cointreau.

After a stroll across the Southern Cotswolds, thirsts can be quenched with a good range of fine ales. These include Flowers Original and Boddingtons, Wadworth 6X and Brand Oak Bitter from nearby Wickwar. It is hardly surprising that the Dog enjoys a roaring trade. The inn does get very busy – especially at weekends – so this is one walk I would definitely recommend at quieter times.

Telephone: 01454 312006.

*How to get there:* The Dog Inn lies on the A432 Chipping Sodbury to Old Sodbury road, a mile before its junction with the A46.

*The ramparts at Sodbury Hillfort.*

*Parking:* There is a car park for patrons alongside the Dog Inn, whilst the two minor roads that join the A432 alongside the inn – Chapel Lane and Cotswold Lane – both offer roadside parking.

*Length of the walk:* 2½ miles. Map: OS Landranger 172 Bristol and Bath (inn GR 754815).

*Old Sodbury lies on the Cotswold Way, deep in the Southern Cotswolds. From the Dog Inn, a 250 ft climb onto the Cotswold plateau brings fine views across the Severn Vale as well as the chance to visit Sodbury hillfort. Enclosing a site of some eleven acres, this multivallate Iron Age fort subsequently played host to both Roman and Saxon armies. The return to Old Sodbury follows the Cotswold Way along the foot of the escarpment. At the entrance to the village stands the picturesque church dedicated to St John the Baptist. The view from the churchyard seats across the Severn to the Welsh Hills brings a memorable end to this delightful stroll in the Southwolds.*

**The Walk**

Cross the road outside the Dog, turn right and follow the pavement alongside the busy A432 for just 50 yards to an unmarked road on the left. Turn left along this road, which runs between a number of houses to reach the village hall. Follow the signposted footpath alongside the hall to an open field, where you head uphill and begin climbing the Cotswold escarpment. Fine views begin to open up behind you across the Severn Vale to Wales. At the top of the field, pass through a gateway and follow an enclosed path to Church Lane. Turn left at the road and, in just a matter of yards, right onto a public footpath signposted to Little Sodbury and Badminton.

The path follows an enclosed course for just 50 yards to a stile on the left. Cross this stile, and head uphill across the field to a clearly visible stile in the opposite hedgerow. Continue along an enclosed path beyond this stile, steadily climbing to reach the Cotswold plateau 250 ft above the Dog Inn back in Old Sodbury. At the top of the climb, the path enters an open hilltop field. Our next target is to reach the hillfort, ½ mile away on the left. Most walkers simply turn left to follow an unofficial footpath to the ancient fortifications, but we will stick to the somewhat circuitous but official right-of-way.

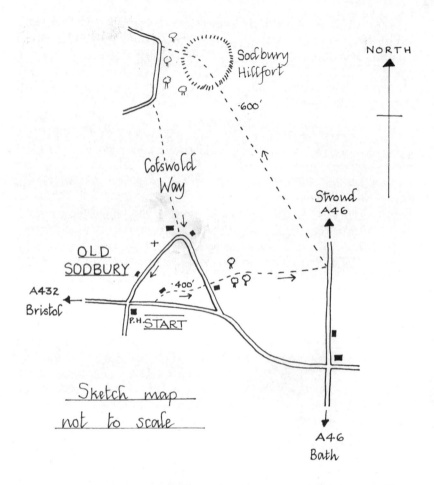

Keep directly ahead, following the right-hand hedgerow for ¼ mile until you reach the A46. Here you do a 135° turn – if you cannot work out the maths, with your back to the main road bear half-right across the large arable field you find yourself in! Aim for a gap halfway down the wall on the opposite side of the field, and continue across to the far left-hand corner of the next field where a pair of stiles give you access to the Sodbury hillfort site.

Cross this enclosure, following the western ramparts of the hillfort, in the direction of a farm. About 200 yards before you reach the farm buildings, look out for a gate/stile down below the

*The path to Sodbury Hillfort*

ramparts on the left. Follow the shady, tree-covered path beyond this stile down to a quiet lane. Turn left and continue along the lane for 150 yards, before bearing left onto a footpath signposted to Old Sodbury. This enclosed path runs along the foot of the escarpment for 300 yards before bearing to the left to climb back up to the hillfort. At this point, leave the main path and cross a stile on the right into a hillside pasture. Follow the well-worn path along the foot of this field for ½ mile to a stile, and a short section of enclosed path that leads down to Cotswold Lane in Old Sodbury. On the right is St John's church, worth a detour to enjoy one final view from the churchyard across the Severn Vale. The route itself continues down Cotswold Lane to the A432 and the Dog Inn.

# 6 Frenchay
## The White Lion

The village of Frenchay maintains a remarkably rural feel, despite being just 5 miles from the centre of Bristol and being bordered by some of the city's eastern suburbs. The village is centred upon a delightful common, overlooked by Georgian merchants' houses, the parish church, the local school and the White Lion. The inn is not of any great antiquity, probably post-dating the church, which itself was only constructed in 1834. Indeed, it is an unremarkable building, most noted for the ornate plaster sculpture on its outside wall depicting a white lion! One local guidebook describes this feature as 'citified Edwardian scrollwork'.

Internally, the White Lion has been extensively modernised in recent years. On entering the inn, there is one long bar area, which leads into a non-smoking alcove and a dining area. The dining area gives access to the inn's pleasant rear garden. The bar areas are carpeted throughout, and comfortably furnished. A tiled fireplace and wood panelling completes the inn's decor. Around the walls are displayed a variety of prints and photographs. Local historians will be attracted by old views of Frenchay Weir and the nearby Old

Cleeve Mill, whilst sports enthusiasts will quickly spot the print of W. G. Grace. The Grace brothers were born in the neighbouring village of Downend, and often played cricket on Frenchay Common. In the mid 19th century, one of the family even managed to hit the church clock with a spectacular six!

The day's dishes are displayed on a blackboard beside the inn's servery area. The options change frequently, but might typically include such favourites as pork and egg pie, various quiches, honey-roast ham, minced beef lasagne, ham and leek pie and ploughman's lunches. On a recent visit, the selections also included cajun sausages and turkey New Orleans, although the availability of these more specialist dishes cannot always be guaranteed. To add insult to injury should you be a weight-watcher, the desserts on offer might include hot chocolate fudge cake, pecan pie and lemon meringue pie.

The White Lion offers a fairly typical range of beers, that includes Theakstons, John Smith's Bitter, Courage Directors and Best Bitter. After a stroll through the nearby Frome Valley, a refreshing pint overlooking Frenchay Common will be the perfect finale to a most pleasant day out in the countryside.

Telephone: 01179 568787.

*How to get there:* Follow the B4058 Iron Acton road out of Bristol as far as the mini-roundabout at the entrance to Frenchay Hospital. Turn right into Begbrook Park and, in just 400 yards, right again along Pearces Hill. In just 150 yards, turn left along The Common, and the White Lion is just a short distance along this turning.

*Parking:* There is a car park opposite the White Lion, on the edge of Frenchay Common, as well as extensive roadside parking in the vicinity of the inn.

*Length of the walk:* 3 miles. Map: OS Landranger 172 Bristol and Bath (inn GR 639773).

*This delightful walk explores a landscape of contrasts – the opulence of Frenchay Common, with its Georgian merchants' houses, cheek by jowl with the workaday world of the nearby Frome Valley. In the 19th century, the valley was a real hive of activity with small-scale quarries, an iron foundry and numerous mills.*

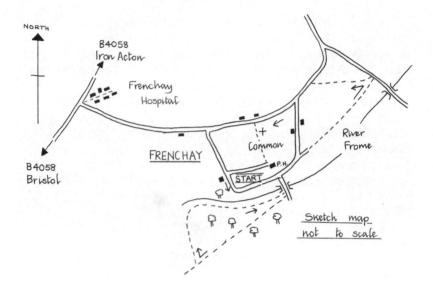

Sketch map
not to scale

*Today, the riverside walk is tranquil and atmospheric, nature reclaiming for herself a small parcel of land on the eastern fringes of Bristol. The name Frome is derived from the Anglo-Saxon 'frum' meaning rapid or vigorous, an apt description for the river which rises in Dodington Park on the Cotswold escarpment and flows in a south-westerly direction for some 20 miles before entering the Floating Harbour in Bristol city centre.*

## The Walk

From the White Lion, walk back to Pearces Hill and turn left. Continue down the hill to the Frome, cross Frenchay Bridge and take the tarmac footpath immediately on the right. In just a few yards, the path forks. Bear left and continue uphill through the trees, as the path passes beneath a series of rock faces. The Frome is below to your right, deep in its wooded valley.

At the top of the climb, the path crosses open parkland before reaching a bridge that crosses a tributary stream of the Frome. Immediately before this bridge, turn right onto a less well defined path that borders the stream down to the river Frome itself. The path crosses a footbridge en route to follow the opposite bank of the stream. When you reach the Frome, turn right and follow the riverside path for ½ mile back to Frenchay Bridge. This is a

*Frenchay Common.*

delightful section of the walk, with the river flowing in a secluded and wooded gorge.

Cross Frenchay Bridge, and turn right into Frenchay Hill. Continue past the old iron works until, in 250 yards, you turn right into Chapel Lane, following the signposted Frome Valley Walkway. The path soon enters an open field, where you follow the well defined fieldpath directly ahead for ¼ mile until you reach a road beside Cleeve Bridge. Ignore one kissing-gate on the left along the way.

Turn left and, in just 20 yards, left again through a kissing-gate giving access to the National Trust's 'Frenchay Moor'. Follow the path as it bears to the right up the slope and through a small copse. Once through the trees, cross the field to a clearly visible kissing-gate and, in the adjoining field, continue in the same direction to a second kissing-gate. This gives access to the fringes of Frenchay Common bordering Beckspool Road.

Follow Beckspool Road to the left, until you reach the main part of Frenchay Common overlooked by the local church. Cross the common to the right of both the church and the village school, and you will find yourself back outside the White Lion.

# 7 Castle Combe
## The White Hart

Castle Combe is undoubtedly one of Britain's most attractive villages. Its golden cottages nestle at the foot of a charming valley, made even more beautiful by the sparkling waters of the By brook. The White Hart stands at the northern end of the village's main street, directly opposite the ancient market cross.

The White Hart is a charming old inn, with its whitewashed walls and stone-tiled roof. Internally, there is one main bar together with a family room, whilst to the rear of the inn is an attractive beer garden with a number of picnic tables. The main bar, with its flagstone flooring and wooden beams, conveys a very rural feel. This effect is enhanced by a fine open fireplace and low ceilings, whilst around the walls are displayed prints, photographs and various items of rural memorabilia. These include a rather fine horse harness and several old cider pots. The adjoining family room is more simply furnished, with a good number of tables and chairs offering ample accommodation for younger visitors.

The White Hart offers a good selection of snacks and bar meals, which are colourfully listed on blackboards alongside the bar. The normal bar fare of salads, sandwiches, steaks and ploughman's lunches is naturally available, together with a number of less traditional offerings. These might typically include king prawns in garlic butter, Cumberland sausages filled with cheese and rolled in bacon, chicken tikka on a bed of rice, deep fried brie and cranberry sauce and red hot chilli con carne. As befits an inn with a family room, children are not forgotten. Their menu runs to all the old favourites – burgers, sausages, eggs, ham and chips – as well as smaller portions of some of the main menu dishes. The sweets available include lemon meringue pie, chocolate fudge cake, apple pie and a selection of ice-creams. The White Hart also offers a good selection of beers and ales. These include offerings from such illustrious brewers as Ushers, Ruddles, Wadworth and Tetley.

Telephone: 01249 782455

*How to get there:* From the village of Ford, 5 miles west of Chippenham on the A420 Bristol road, an unclassified road is signposted to Castle Combe. Follow this lane through the village to the market cross, opposite which lies the White Hart inn.

*Parking:* There is no car park at the White Hart, and only room for a few cars on the roadside outside the pub. If you continue out of the village for 200 yards, there is roadside parking for a number of vehicles on the right-hand side of the road.

*Length of the walk:* 3 miles. Map: OS Landranger 173 Swindon and Devizes (inn GR 843772).

*Castle Combe has the unenviable distinction of being arguably Britain's prettiest village. The golden cottages alongside the By brook must have featured on thousands of jigsaw puzzles, paintings, guidebooks and cards, giving the village an air of familiarity to even the first-time visitor. The castle in the place-name is a motte and bailey construction, sadly lying on private land. This walk, however, does give the opportunity to explore the combe that lends its name to the village. Deep in this sheltered wooded valley, our steps border Broadmead brook, crossed at one point by an ancient clapper bridge. Back in the village, look out for the trout almost motionless in By brook, as well as the faceless clock in St Andrew's church.*

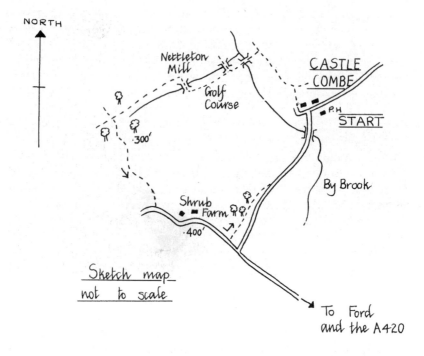

NORTH

Nettleton Mill

Golf Course

CASTLE COMBE

P.H

START

300'

By Brook

Shrub Farm

400'

Sketch map
not to scale

To Ford
and the A420

*Castle Combe is unpleasantly crowded at peak times – please try
and visit the village on a quiet weekday outside the holiday period!*

## The Walk

Follow the cul-de-sac opposite the White Hart, past the Castle Inn
and under the archway built into an old cottage. In 100 yards,
where this lane ends, continue uphill along an enclosed footpath
until you reach a stile. Beyond this stile, turn left and follow another
enclosed path downhill until it emerges onto the local golf course.
Follow the signposted path past the greens, crossing By brook on a
stone bridge very early on. In 200 yards, just before a second bridge
across the river, turn left onto a signposted path that leaves the golf
course to head into the adjoining woodland.

This delightfully secluded path borders Broadmead brook on its
way to Nettleton Mill. Just before the mill, pass through a kissing-
gate on the right and cross the stream. The path bears left between
the first two groups of buildings you pass, and continues through
Deverell's Plantation for ¼ mile until you reach a gate/stile. Turn

*Castle Combe.*

left along the bridlepath just beyond this gateway, cross the ancient clapper bridge across the river and continue along the enclosed path for ½ mile until you reach a quiet lane.

Turn left along this lane and, in 300 yards, you will pass the first of two drives on the left leading to Shrub Farm. The second entrance follows in 150 yards, beyond which the lane borders Becker's Wood on the left. In another 150 yards, look out for a wooden stile leading into this woodland. Cross this stile, and follow the path as it bears to the left into the heart of Becker's Wood. The path follows a level course for 400 yards, before descending steeply to join the lane leading into Castle Combe. Turn left at the road, which shortly borders By brook before crossing the old packhorse bridge at the approach to the village's main street. Continue past the picturesque cottages up to the market cross, St Andrew's church and the White Hart.

# 8 Cold Ashton
## The White Hart

High on the Cotswold escarpment, the village of Cold Ashton enjoys a most spectacular location overlooking St Catherine's Valley. The White Hart stands apart from the village, on the old coach road running from Bristol to London. The history of the inn, however, predates the era of the stage coach by more than 150 years.

There has been a hostelry on this site since 1600, when the large stone residence served as a local brewhouse to the villagers. In 1643, following a Civil War skirmish at nearby Lansdown, wounded royalist soldiers were carried back to the White Hart for treatment. The stage coach era saw the White Hart serving as a staging post on the route from Bristol to London, with the highwayman Captain Spindrift a well-known face in the neighbourhood! During the Napoleonic Wars, a gang of French prisoners of war was based at the inn, whilst they worked on improving the local road network. In the mid 19th century, Ushers acquired the White Hart and 35 acres of land for the princely sum of £1,978 13s 8d making it one of the oldest houses in their empire.

As soon as you walk into the White Hart, it is evident that this is indeed an inn with a true sense of history. Exposed stonework, dark wood beams, old fireplaces, rural prints, copper and brassware all combine to give the inn a very traditional feel. Around the walls are displayed a number of shields, accompanied by swords, axes and even a shotgun! More recently, the bar area has been divided up into a number of more intimate areas with the clever use of beams as partitions, adding to the warmth of the hostelry.

The menu at the White Hart covers starters, grills, house specials, salads, vegetarian dishes, bar snacks and sweets. The house specials will certainly appeal, and include roast Scotch beef, Squire's gammon, venison, duck and bacon and Somerset chicken. This last dish consists of fresh tender sliced chicken, apples and onions in a cider sauce. The sweets – which are all served with lashings of fresh cream – include gateaux, raspberry surprise, chocolate nut sundae and hot chocolate fudge cake.

To the rear of the White Hart is a large, well kept garden, where youngsters can amuse themselves on the various items of play equipment. It really is just the place to enjoy a refreshing pint after a

*Monkswood reservoir.*

fairly stiff walk through the nearby St Catherine's Valley. To quench your thirst, the White Hart offers such beers as Ushers Bitter, Courage Bitter, Websters and Wadworth 6X.

Telephone: 01225 891233.

*How to get there:* The White Hart lies on the A420, midway between Bristol and Chippenham, and just ½ mile east of its junction with the A46.

*Parking:* There is a large car park for patrons at the White Hart. Room for roadside parking in the immediate vicinity of the inn is very limited. If you cannot find space, drive back to the junction with the A46, turn left towards Bath and take the first turning left into the village to park alongside the church. The church is just five minutes' walk from the White Hart.

*Length of the walk:* 3 miles. Map: OS Landranger 172 Bristol and Bath (inn GR 749730).

*Cold Ashton is a delightful Cotswold village, centred upon a quiet byway. The manor house, the rectory, the church and the old school all follow each other in quick succession along the north side of the village street, casting their gaze southwards across St Catherine's Valley. The valley is delightfully secluded, and carries a diminutive stream down to its confluence with the river Avon at Batheaston. This walk explores the village, before plunging into the valley below. The landscape is superb – woodland, steep hillsides, grazing rather than arable farming and scarcely a building in sight. The walk also provides the opportunity to visit Monkswood Reservoir, source of much of Bath's water supply. The two or three stiff climbs are but a small price to pay for the rewards of what must be one of the best walks in the area.*

**The Walk**

Follow the signposted Cotswold Way across the road from the White Hart. It runs down to Cold Ashton church, before joining Hyde Lane through the village. Turn left along this road and, 100 yards past the last cottage in Cold Ashton, follow a signposted footpath on the right-hand side. The path passes through a gateway, before heading down the left-hand side of a field to a

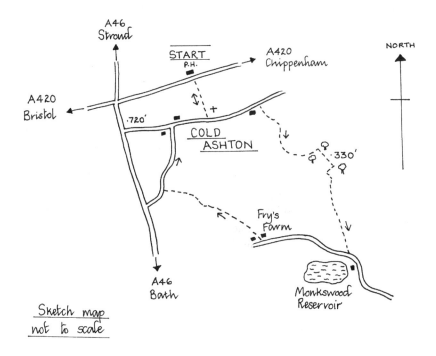

gate in the bottom corner. In the next field, continue down the left-hand boundary to another gate, all the while enjoying the fine views across St Catherine's Valley.

Beyond this gateway, follow a sunken, enclosed path ahead for just 100 yards to a gate. Continue following the path as it gradually bears to the left along the foot of a steep slope. In 600 yards, look out for a gate/stile in the hedgerow on your right. Cross the stile, and head downhill – keeping to the left of some bramble bushes – until you reach a diminutive stone footbridge crossing St Catherine's brook. Once across the stream, follow the footpath uphill to the right, keeping a line of trees to your left. In 100 yards, you will reach a stile where the path enters an open field.

Once through an area of bracken and into the open pasture, turn left and follow a fieldpath across the hillside. The path is occasionally indistinct – the key point is to keep to the level as the path contours around the hillside. In 350 yards, the path reaches a gate/stile. Follow the track beyond this stile for 600 yards until it joins the lane running through the valley.

*Cold Ashton Manor.*

A detour to the left down the hill will bring you to Monkswood Reservoir. The main walk turns right, and follows the lane for ½ mile as far as Fry's Farm. Turn right between the farmhouse and the adjacent barns, and follow an enclosed bridlepath across the hill for just under ½ mile to an open field, with the views extending across to Cold Ashton on the hilltop. Head across this field to a gateway opposite and, in the next field, follow the bridlepath across to the opposite hedgerow. Follow the path alongside this hedge to the right, up to a gateway and Slough Lane.

Turn right, and follow Slough Lane uphill back into Cold Ashton. Turn right at the junction with Hyde Lane, and walk past the manor and the rectory to the parish church. Follow the path up to the church, and continue across the field to reach the A420 and the White Hart.

# **Bathford**
## ⑨ The Crown

Driving along the London Road out of Bath, the wooded slopes of Bathford Hill dominate the landscape, with Brown's Folly standing magnificently on the hilltop. Nestling at the foot of the hillside is the attractive village of Bathford, site of an ancient crossing point across a tributary stream of the river Avon. Literally the first building one passes on reaching the village is the Crown, fronting onto a wide expanse of road that was once the terminus of a local tram service running to the village from the centre of Bath. With the village climbing away from the Crown on a 1-in-5 gradient, this was the logical place for the tram service to stop!

The Crown is laid out in an attractive manner, with a series of rooms connected to a central bar area. The furnishings range from formal dining sets through to relaxing armchairs, ensuring that every conceivable customer taste is catered for. With its stripped and polished floorboards, rugs, log fire, prints, photos, china and stoneware, the Crown possesses a traditional atmosphere that is very much in keeping with its origins back in the mid 18th century.

All sizes of appetites will find something to their liking at the

*Bathford church.*

Crown. Lighter snacks on offer include rolls, soup, toasted sandwiches, baked potatoes and ploughman's lunches. Heartier appetites might extend to such tempting options as steak, mushroom and ale pie, venison pie, trout, chicken Kiev, lentil nut casserole or seafood pancakes. Children are well catered for with their own menu. The climb to Brown's Folly will in all probability have given you quite an appetite. The fine range of desserts, including Dutch brandy cake and toffee butterscotch pudding, will therefore prove most welcome. The prices are not cheap, but meals are generous and well prepared.

The beers available at the Crown include Bass, Marston's Pedigree and Ushers. The wine list is fairly extensive, too, and includes a number of interesting English country wines. A chilled glass of wine or a cool beer, sampled in the Crown's garden, will prove most welcome following this short but strenuous walk onto Bathford Hill.

Telephone: 01225 852297.

*How to get there:* Follow the A4 London road out of Bath for 2 miles to its junction with the A363 Bradford-on-Avon road. Just 100 yards along the A363, fork left onto Bathford Hill. Almost straightaway, the Crown will be seen on the right-hand side of the road.

*Parking:* There is a small parking area for patrons immediately in front of the Crown. As this is usually full, most cars are parked on the roadside in the immediate vicinity of the inn.

*Length of the walk:* 2 miles. Map: OS Landranger 172 Bristol and Bath (inn GR 787669).

*Brown's Folly, high on Bathford Hill, is a well known landmark to most Bathonians. The tower was commissioned in 1849 by Mr Wade-Brown, a local quarry owner, allegedly to promote the quality of his building stone! Beneath the folly are a maze of underground passages, from where much of the stone used in the construction of Georgian Bath was extracted. In the shadow of the tower lies the village of Bathford, with many of its old buildings fashioned from local stone. The quarry workers would have lived in the artisans' cottages that lie scattered across the hillside. This short walk climbs the 600 ft from the village to Brown's Folly, passing through Brown's Folly Nature Reserve, an area of mixed woodland, scrub and limestone grass that has grown over the remains of the former quarries. The rich flora and fauna includes badgers, slow-worms, harebells, rockrose, woolly thistle and agrimony.*

*Although short on miles, this is an extremely strenuous walk that is better suited to active youngsters than toddlers.*

**The Walk**

Follow the pavement up Bathford Hill for 350 yards until you reach Bathford post office. Leave the main road, and follow the lane that runs immediately to the right of the post office. This lane ends at a footpath, which is followed for a short distance up to Dovers Park. Cross this road, and follow the cul-de-sac lane opposite. In 300 yards, the lane reaches a stile. Cross the stile, and follow the path directly ahead across the hillside. In 250 yards, it passes a rank of cottages on the left before joining the Bathford to Monkton Farleigh road. The stiff climb up from the Crown has the reward of expansive views across the By Brook valley towards Colerne, perched on the opposite hillside.

Follow the signposted footpath immediately to your right, that runs alongside a house before entering the Brown's Folly Nature Reserve. The enclosed path climbs up through the woodland for 300 yards, before reaching a prominent gravel track. Turn right, and follow this track for just 50 yards before bearing left onto a less well defined path that climbs the hillside. In 150 yards, this path emerges into a clearing on the hillside, from where the views across the Avon Valley towards Bath are quite exceptional.

As you enter this clearing, look out for a series of wooden steps on the left. Climb these steps to the top of the hillside, where you meet a cross-track. Turn right, and follow this path for just 200 yards to another clearing alongside Brown's Folly. The views again are quite magnificent and, as this point marks the end of the climbing, a well deserved rest is probably in order!

Continue along the hilltop path past the tower for 200 yards, before turning right by a marker post to follow a series of steps down the hillside. At the foot of these steps, turn right along a track for just 30 yards, before forking left to follow a path down the hillside back towards Bathford. In 100 yards, this path meets a forestry track. Turn right along this track for just 15 yards, before

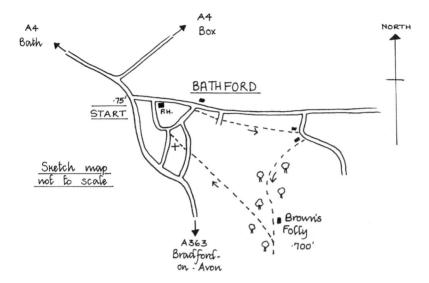

bearing to the left to continue along the footpath leading back to Bathford. This path descends through the woodland for 200 yards before reaching a stile, the exit point from Brown's Folly Nature Reserve.

Cross the open field beyond this stile to the stile opposite, just to the right of a telegraph pole. Cross this stile, and bear left down to Pump Lane. Opposite are a pair of cottages – Milk Wood Cottage and Manor Farm Cottage. Follow the alley that runs beside Manor Farm Cottage down to Church Lane and St Swithin's church. Follow the lane opposite – the unmarked Ostlings Lane – back downhill. In 300 yards, it joins Bathford Hill alongside the Crown.

# 10 Lacock
# The George Inn

Lacock has been described as 'easily the most remarkable and most beautiful village in Wiltshire'. Based around four streets – Church Street, West and East Streets and the High Street – Lacock still very much resembles a medieval town. The George, the oldest inn in Lacock and dating from 1361, overlooks West Street near its junction with the High Street. As if to remind the visitor that Lacock sits at the geological divide between limestone country and the clay vale of the Avon, the inn is constructed of an appealing mix of Bath stone and local red bricks.

Stone-mullioned windows, low beams and occasional flagstones hint at the great age of the George. This historical feel is further enhanced by upright timbers that have replaced knocked-through walls, and an exceptional central fireplace burning with a log fire during the cold winter months. Encased in the outer breast of this fireplace is a three-ft treadwheel. For many years a dog was placed within the treadwheel to power the inn's turnspit! Customers enjoying hospitality at the George can relax in the inn's Windsor chairs and armchairs, or alternatively sun themselves in the attractive rear garden. All tastes should find something to their liking on the inn's menu. In addition to pub staples like sandwiches, stick rolls, ploughman's lunches and salads, the George offers such tasty dishes as chicken, leek and Stilton, smoked trout, broccoli and cream cheese bake and steak and kidney pie. Designed to replace those calories burned off walking beside the river Avon earlier in the day are desserts such as spotted dick and rhubarb crumble.

To accompany your meal, the George offers a selection of fine Wadworth beers from nearby Devizes. These might typically include Farmer's Glory and Henry's Original IPA, as well as the brewery's flagship, the magnificent 6X. What could be better than one of Wiltshire's best beers in one of the county's oldest inns!

Telephone: 01249 730263.

*How to get there:* Lacock lies just ½ mile off the main A350 Chippenham to Melksham road, halfway between these two towns. The George Inn faces onto West Street, just north of its junction with Lacock's High Street.

*Reybridge.*

*Parking:* As well as a car park for patrons, there is ample room for parking on West Street in the vicinity of the George.

*Length of the walk:* 2½ miles. Map: OS Landranger 173 Swindon and Devizes (inn GR 915685).

*Lacock, deep in the Wiltshire countryside, is a National Trust village of international repute. The medieval street plan, the local abbey, the church and a host of magnificent buildings attract thousands of visitors each year. Whilst the village itself could easily fill several hours of your time, this walk also provides the opportunity to explore the river Avon as it meanders across the local floodplain from Reybridge.*

## The Walk

Turn right outside the George, and walk the short distance along West Street to its junction with Lacock's High Street. Turn into the High Street, and continue for ½ mile through Lacock and out onto the Devizes road. Just past the abbey grounds, the pavement becomes a raised causeway before reaching a stone bridge across the Avon.

Once across the river, cross a stone slab stile on the left-hand side to follow a signposted footpath into an open field. On the far side of this field, a couple of telegraph poles stand alongside the hedgerow. Aim for the right-hand telegraph pole, alongside which sits a stile. Cross this stile, and follow the left-hand hedgerow in the next field to another stile. Beyond this stile, follow the telegraph wires across the next field to a gateway. Down below this gateway, the path joins the banks of the river Avon.

Follow the riverbank through to Reybridge, where the river is crossed by way of an attractive stone bridge. Once across the river, turn left in front of a pair of thatched cottages. In just 20 yards, where the road bears to the right, follow the tarmac path ahead between a pair of cottages to reach an open field. A tarmac path crosses this field to Lacock, with fine views of the river Avon and Bowden Hill away to the left.

Pass through a gate on the far side of the field, and turn left along a path that leads into Lacock. This path crosses Bide brook before

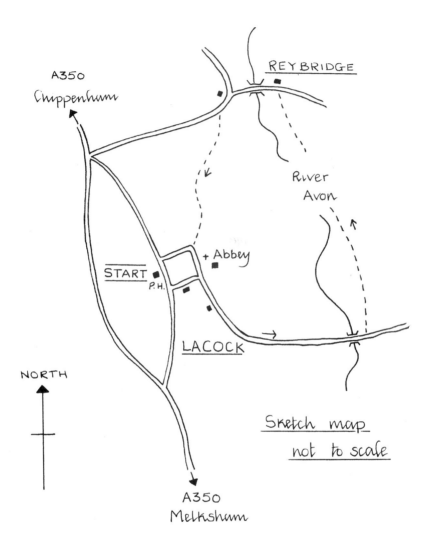

A350
Chippenham

REYBRIDGE

River
Avon

START
P.H.

+ Abbey

LACOCK

NORTH

Sketch map
not to scale

A350
Melksham

reaching the parish church. Turn right just by the church, and continue along Church Street to its junction with West Street. A left turn will soon return you to the George.

# 11 Winsley
## The Seven Stars

The Seven Stars, a fine old inn crafted of the local Bath stone, lies alongside the main road in the heart of old Winsley. Many a passing motorist must be drawn by this appealing hostelry, with its courtyard tables usually busy in the summer months with customers enjoying a refreshing pint. Visitors will not be disappointed.

Internally, there is an L-shaped bar area, with beams, open fireplaces and exposed stonework giving the inn a most traditional feel. Scattered around the various alcoves are darkwood tables and chairs, and high-backed settles, fully complementing the Seven Stars' general decor. Around the walls are displayed brasses and plates, together with a number of attractive prints featuring rural landscapes and animals, as well as canal scenes. The inn possesses what one guidebook has described as a 'cosy sitting-room effect'.

Each day, the menu is displayed on a board just inside the bar area. On a recent visit, the dishes included home-made soup, smoked trout, gala pie, ploughman's lunches, pork and apple pie, quiche, ham and pineapple and plaice. Although there is not a specific child's menu, an adult portion and a spare plate will suffice for a couple of hungry youngsters!

A number of mainstream real ales are always available at the Seven Stars, including Bass, Wadworth 6X, Old Speckled Hen and Marston's Pedigree. Good beers, wholesome food and a delightful country inn, at the end of an exhilarating walk in the Avon Valley – the perfect combination!

Telephone: 01225 722204.

*How to get there:* Follow the A36 south from Bath for 6 miles to its junction with the B3108 Bradford-on-Avon road. Follow this 'B' road towards Bradford and, in just 2 miles, you will find the Seven Stars on the roadside in the heart of Winsley.

*Parking:* There is a car park for patrons beside the Seven Stars. Roadside parking is also available alongside St Nicholas' church in Winsley – continue along the road towards Bradford for just a few yards, and turn left just before the main road bears sharply to the right.

*Length of the walk:* 2 miles. Maps: OS Landranger 172 Bath and Bristol and 173 Swindon and Devizes will both be needed for this walk (inn GR 799609).

*Although dominated by modern housing, the old core of Winsley still possesses a traditional village feel. It is worth spending a little time exploring the area around the church before heading south from the village into the nearby Avon Valley. The walk descends the steep hillside above the Avon, to reach the Kennet and Avon Canal. The towpath is followed through to the secluded hamlet of Avoncliff, with its noted aqueduct, before the climb back up into Winsley. Pleasing landscapes, a restored canal, rich flora and fauna and expansive views make this an almost perfect short walk.*

**The Walk**

Follow the pavement beside the B3108 towards Bath for just 50 yards. Where the main road bears right, continue straight ahead along a cul-de-sac that runs beside the local bowling club. This lane very quickly bears left, and then right, before reaching a house called The Chase View. Just before this house, cross a stone stile in

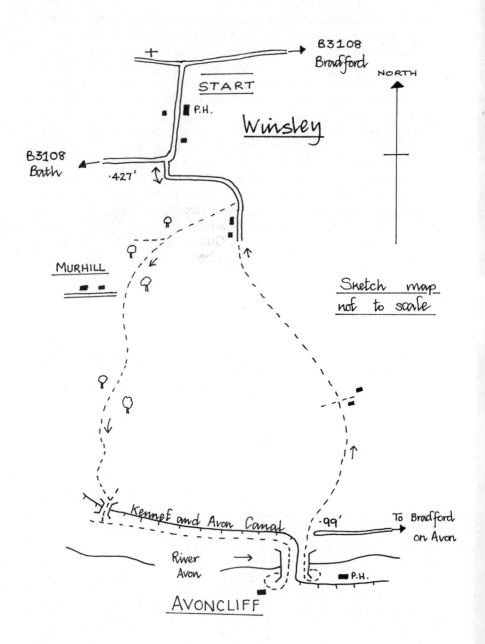

B3108
Bradford

NORTH

START

P.H.

Winsley

B3108
Bath

·427'

MURHILL

Sketch map
not to scale

Kennet and Avon Canal

·99'

To Bradford
on Avon

River
Avon

P.H.

AVONCLIFF

the wall on the right. Follow the enclosed footpath down to a stile and a flight of steps. Just past the stile, the path divides. Follow the left-hand footpath as it heads downhill to reach a lane in the secluded hamlet of Murhill.

Do not follow the lane to the right, rather continue ahead along the footpath as it heads downhill deep into the Avon Valley. The path ends at a stile, where you cross the open hillside pasture ahead to a second stile at the foot of the slope. Turn right along the track beyond this stile, cross the Kennet and Avon Canal and drop down to the towpath on the left. Follow this towpath along the valley bottom for ½ mile into Avoncliff.

The towpath bears sharply to the right to cross the river Avon by means of the local aqueduct. Once across this fine construction, follow the steps down on the right-hand side and pass under the aqueduct to emerge by the Cross Guns pub. Walk back up to the canal, turn right and follow the path back across the aqueduct – on the opposite side this time! – to reach a small parking area.

Do not follow the road out of Avoncliff to the right – instead, follow the footpath directly ahead that climbs a series of steps to reach a kissing-gate and an open field. Follow the fieldpath uphill to the top right-hand corner of this hillside pasture, enjoying the fine views of Avoncliff tucked away deep in the valley below. At the top of this field, cross the track and pass through the kissing-gate opposite. An enclosed path is then followed up the hill back into Winsley.

At the top of the hill, the path reaches a stile alongside Winsley Cricket Club. The views from the hilltop are exceptional, along the valley to nearby Bradford-on-Avon and out as far as the Westbury White Horse on the edge of Salisbury Plain. Continue along the lane beyond this stile, which shortly passes The Chase View and the local bowling club to rejoin the B3108. A right turn at the main road returns you to the Seven Stars.

# 12 Southstoke
## The Packhorse

The Packhorse inn at Southstoke dates back well over 400 years, and has lost very little of its sense of history as the 20th century has progressed. The lane outside the inn was once a packhorse trail. Thirsty horsemen, having climbed the slopes from Midford and Combe Hay, would have paused at the Packhorse for a welcome pint or two. The central passage leading through this magnificent gabled stone building was originally a right of way to the local church. In centuries past the dead would have made their last journey literally through the pub to their resting place!

Internally, the Packhorse is as old and unspoilt as the exterior. There are stone and quarry-tiled floors, open fireplaces, beam-and-plank ceilings, oak settles, captain's chairs and rough black window shutters. I particularly like the story that is told about the cupboard inside the vast inglenook fireplace. This was allegedly where the drunks were locked away until they had sobered up.

The Packhorse offers a range of traditional pub food that represents excellent value for customers. The dishes range from filled rolls, ploughman's lunches and pasties, through to steak pie, fisherman's pie and sausage plait. To accompany your meal, a pint of Ushers Best Bitter or Founders comes particularly recommended, as does a glass of local West Country cider. On warm days, your food and drink can be enjoyed in the inn's grassed garden, where youngsters can enjoy the swings whilst older folk can simply linger and appreciate the views of the village church.

For a somewhat up-market village less than 1 mile from the suburbs of Bath, the Packhorse will come as a real surprise to lovers of the traditional English pub. Customers have been spared the terrible excesses of modernisation and innovation, leaving a fine old inn that the packhorse drivers from the 18th and 19th centuries would quickly recognise as their favourite watering-hole.

Telephone: 01225 832060.

*How to get there:* 2 miles south of Bath, leave the A367 Radstock road to follow the B3110 towards Midford. Just 1 mile from the A367, an unclassified road is signposted to Southstoke. As you enter the village, turn sharp left by a telephone box to follow a lane down to the Packhorse inn.

*Parking:* There is a small car park for patrons in front of the Packhorse. Careful roadside parking is also possible in the vicinity of the inn. A particularly good place to park is alongside the telephone box as you enter the village, just 100 yards up the hill from the Packhorse.

*Length of the walk:* 3 miles. Map: OS Landranger 172 Bristol and Bath (inn GR 747613).

*Southstoke is an attractive stone village, clinging to the hillside above a secluded valley carrying Cam brook to its confluence with the Avon. Hidden away in the valley are the decaying remains of the Somerset Coal Canal, the lifeline that in the 19th century linked the collieries of the North Somerset Coalfield with their markets across southern England. The highlight of the circuit will undoubtedly be the Combe Hay Locks hidden away in Engine Wood. This flight of 22 locks lifted the canal up a 154 ft rise between Midford and Combe Hay. In the middle of this flight of locks lies the Bull's Nose, almost certainly the only horseshoe bend on the British canal network.*

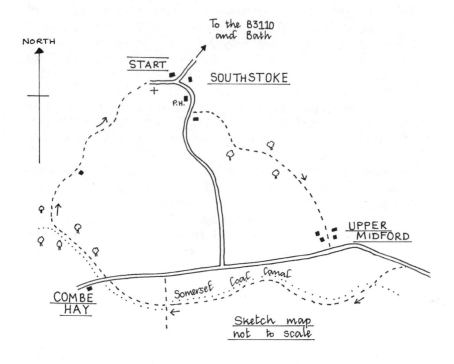

## The Walk

Head down the hill outside the Packhorse for just a few yards until, immediately past the village hall, you turn left onto a signposted footpath. This runs in front of a rank of cottages before bearing right to continue as a shady enclosed path down the hillside. In 400 yards, at a stile, the path enters an open field.

Follow the left-hand hedgerow downhill, keeping to the bottom of a valley, to a stile. Cross the next, much smaller, field to a second stile beyond which the path continues along the bottom of the valley towards Upper Midford. On the edge of this hamlet, cross a stile on the left just past a barn, and follow a driveway past several cottages down to the Midford to Combe Hay road.

Turn left and, in 200 yards, cross a stile on the right just past Hyver Kennels. Drop down to the bed of the long disused Somerset Coal Canal (SCC), and turn right, following the canal bed past an old stone overbridge and onto a railway embankment marking the course of the now defunct Camerton Railway. Cross a stile, bear left

58

and follow a path beneath a railway viaduct to rejoin the bed of the SCC on the far side of the embankment.

Follow the old canal bed through the Cam Brook valley until, in ½ mile, a stile is crossed to join a track coming down from Twinhoe. Turn right for just a few yards, cross a stile on the left and follow a footpath that continues along the course of the SCC. In 200 yards, this path passes through a complex of farm buildings to join the Combe Hay lane.

Cross the road, pass under the Camerton Railway and follow the path ahead beside the Combe Hay Locks for ¼ mile. At the Bull's Nose, where the SCC does a sharp U-turn, cross the stile directly ahead and follow the path leading away from the canal. This path soon begins to climb the hillside towards an isolated cottage. The path passes to the left of this cottage and continues for 100 yards before reaching another open field. Head uphill to a squeeze-belly stile at the top of the field, where a concrete drive is joined that leads back to Manor Farm on the edge of Southstoke. The footpath on the right, immediately past the church, leads back to the Packhorse.

*Southstoke.*

# **Priston**
## The Ring o' Bells

**13**

Priston is not one of those villages that the traveller would naturally stumble upon. Lying a mile below the nearest 'B' road, deep in the valley that carries the Newton brook, the old adage about being 'off the beaten track' would certainly apply here. At the far end of the village, adjoining the village hall, lies the Ring o' Bells.

Constructed of local stone, this is a true village local. Beyond the entrance porch lie the comfortable lounge and public bars, with traditional wooden beams and an abundance of renovated stonework lending a timeless feel to the hostelry. The Ring o' Bells is furnished with cushioned settles, stools and window seats, with a number of dark wood tables scattered throughout both bars. Name tags adorn the walls in odd corners of the pub, with 'Farmer's Den' being self-explanatory, whilst 'Tom and Harry' is the preserve of a pair of village locals! A case of stuffed pheasants and a fine pair of bullock's horns leave the visitor in no doubt that this is farming country.

Other than the usual pub snacks – crisps, nuts and confectionery – food is not available at the Ring o' Bells. This will appeal to conventional drinkers who must resent the fact that many pubs nowadays appear to be little more than glorified restaurants. Being a freehouse, it is not always easy to predict what beers will be available. On a recent visit, the Dorset brewer Hall and Woodhouse featured prominently, with their Badgers Best Bitter and Tanglefoot both being available. Also on tap were Draught Bass and Beamish Irish Stout.

A few tables and chairs are placed outside the Ring o' Bells, giving a good view of Priston's main street. This is the ideal spot to enjoy a quiet beer following an exploration of the hill country to the north of the village.

Telephone: 01761 471467.

*How to get there:* Follow the A367 road from Bath towards Radstock. A couple of miles beyond the city's southern outskirts, turn onto the B3115 signposted to Timsbury. Just 1 mile along this road, in the hamlet of Longhouse, follow the unclassified lane signposted to Priston. In 1 mile, at the western end of the village, lies the Ring o' Bells.

*Priston Mill.*

*Parking:* There is room for roadside parking in the vicinity of the Ring o' Bells, particularly outside the neighbouring village hall.

*Length of the walk:* 3½ miles. Map: OS Landranger 172 Bristol and Bath (inn GR 693605)

*To the south-west of Bath lies a series of rolling hills and deep valleys, each sheltering its own diminutive watercourse. Scattered across this rural landscape is a collection of small villages – Priston, Inglesbatch and Wilmington – traditional farming communities that worked the land in this former corner of North Somerset. Most of the agricultural families have gone, replaced by city commuters, but the area still has a strong attachment to the soil. This is best illustrated by Priston Mill, whose 25-ft diameter overshot water wheel is powered by the waters of Conygre brook. This corn mill has been supplying flour to Bath for over 1,000 years, since it was bequeathed to the city's monks in AD 931. A relatively strenuous walk explores this delightfully rural landscape, with time allowed along the way for a visit to the fully restored water mill.*

**The Walk**
Turn right outside the Ring o' Bells, and walk through Priston to the eastern edge of the village. Just past Willow Barn, cross a stile on the left to follow a signposted footpath towards a water-board installation. Follow the path to the left of this complex, and continue along the edge of two fields just above Newton brook. In the far corner of the second field, cross a footbridge on the right before heading uphill towards Inglesbatch. Aim for the metal barn at the left-hand edge of the village, where the fieldpath joins a bridlepath.

Turn right, and continue into Inglesbatch, bearing left by Home Farm before reaching the centre of the village. Turn left at the telephone box, and continue to the northern edge of the village. Two byways turn off on the left in quick succession, at a point where the village street bears sharply to the right. Follow the first of these byways, as it passes between cottages. In 150 yards, just past the last house in Inglesbatch, this lane becomes an unmetalled bridlepath. Continue along this path for 1 mile to reach the neighbouring hamlet of Wilmington. The path descends steeply to

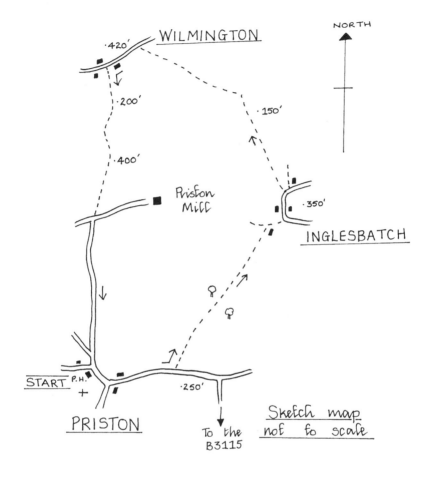

NORTH

WILMINGTON

·420'

·200'

·400'

·150'

Priston Mill

·350'

INGLESBATCH

START  P.H.

PRISTON

·250'

To the B3115

Sketch map
not to scale

cross Newton brook, before climbing a 250 ft rise into Wilmington itself.

Turn left when you join the lane in Wilmington. In just 50 yards, cross a stile on the left and follow a signposted footpath to a stile on the opposite side of a small paddock. Descend the steep hillside beyond this stile, bearing slightly to the right, to reach a stile and wooden footbridge at the bottom of the hillside. Cross the stream, and climb the hillside beyond to reach a stile almost in the top right-hand corner of the field. It is worth pausing at this stile, not only to regain your breath but also to enjoy the view back towards Wilmington.

Head directly across the next field to a gateway opposite, beyond which you can cross the stile on the right-hand side. Drop downhill to a stile in the hedgerow below, and then continue to the far corner of the next field where a gate brings you onto a lane.

A detour to the left will enable you to visit Priston Mill – fee payable but excellent cream teas! The return to Priston involves forking left at the junction immediately to hand, and continuing along this quiet lane for ½ mile back to the village. A left turn at a junction on the edge of Priston will soon see you facing the Ring o' Bells.

*The church at Priston.*

# 14 Swineford
## The Swan

The roadside settlement of Swineford, alongside the river Avon to the west of Bath, does indeed have associations with pigs. A certain Prince Bladud was banished by his father on account of his being a leper. He became a swineherd at Keynsham, just along the river from Swineford, where he passed on his unfortunate complaint to the pigs. Fearing the wrath of his employer, he drove the pigs across shallows in the river. The pigs decided to swim upstream to Bath, where a frolic in the riverside silt and mud deposits cured their leprosy. Bladud took to the mud with the same success, and later built baths over the curative springs for which Bath became famous. This is the legend to muse over as you enjoy your pint in the local inn, just across the meadow from the site of those shallows that lent their name to Swineford.

The Swan, a traditional inn fashioned from the local sandstone, sits alongside the A431 Bath to Bitton road. Internally, there is a public bar, a lounge/dining area and a rear games room. With its half-timbered walls, elements of exposed stonework and stone fireplace, the Swan enjoys a comfortable atmosphere. Around the walls are displayed a number of prints, as well as cigarette cards, Pooh Bear postcards and photographs of the Swineford area. A set of rules from 1786 relating to conduct in public hostelries particularly catches the eye:

'No slap an' tickle o' the wenches
No cockfighting
Flintlocks, cudgels, daggers and swords
to be handed to the innkeeper.'

The Swan offers a typical selection of pub food. Beyond the staples such as thick soup, ploughman's lunches, jacket potatoes, omelettes and hot dogs, patrons can enjoy various steaks, a vast mixed grill, chicken nuggets, chilli or pizza. With the local link with Prince Bladud and his famous pigs, it was disappointing not to see pork and apple sauce on the menu!

The beers and ciders available might typically include Hardington's Bitter, Oakhill Bitter, Otter Bitter and Broadoak Cider. Hardington Brewery was set up as recently as 1991 in South Bristol, and its Best Bitter has been described as 'a crisp, refreshing amber beer ... moreish!'

*River Avon.*

Families are welcome to enjoy the hospitality at the Swan, either in the lounge/dining area or in the beer garden. Following a leisurely stroll by the nearby Avon, a pint of Hardington's in the pub's back garden basking in the summer sun sounds rather pleasant.

Telephone: 01179 323101.

*How to get there:* The roadside settlement of Swineford is just 4 miles west of Bath, on the A431 Bitton and Hanham road. The Swan lies alongside the main road in the centre of the village.

*Parking:* There is a lay-by directly opposite the Swan which is used by the inn's patrons as well as local fishermen. The Swineford Picnic Area is just west of the Swan, and provides further parking spaces.

*Length of the walk:* 3 miles. Map: OS Landranger 172 Bristol and Bath (inn GR 691690).

*To the west of Bath, the Cotswold Hills come tumbling down towards the banks of the river Avon. This relatively gentle circuit provides pleasant walking on the hillsides above Swineford, before returning along the banks of the Avon itself. Along the way lie the villages of Upton Cheyney and Bitton, as well as a section of the old railway that ran between Bristol and Bath Green Park. The line was closed by Dr Beeching in the 1960s, before becoming one of the country's first cycle/walkways. This is a surprisingly rural excursion given the proximity to both Bristol and Bath.*

## The Walk

Turn right outside the Swan, following the A431 towards Bitton. In just 75 yards, turn right onto an unmetalled road signposted to the local picnic area. This roadway passes through a farm complex before reaching the picnic area car park. Over on the left-hand side of the grassed picnic area, look out for a stile. Cross this stile, bear right and follow the right-hand field boundary uphill through two fields. At the end of the second field, continue along the path ahead – it runs along the left-hand edge of the next field – to reach a lane leading into Upton Cheyney.

Turn right and, in 200 yards, immediately past the Upton Inn, turn

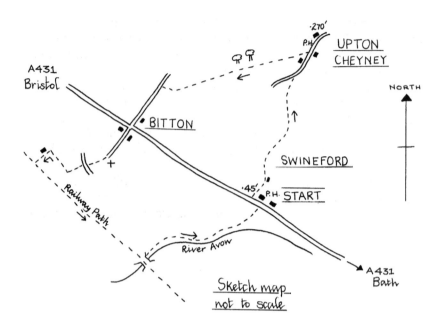

Sketch map
not to scale

left onto a footpath signposted to Bitton. This unmetalled lane soon
reaches a gateway and open fields. Head downhill to a squeeze-
belly stile at the foot of the slope, before continuing along a short
enclosed section of path to a stile on the left. Cross this stile, bear
right and follow the hedge to a gate in the corner of the field.
Continue along a well-worn fieldpath in the next field to a gate
opposite, before crossing one final field to reach a metal stile and
housing on the edge of Bitton. Bear right along the enclosed path
behind the first group of houses to reach Golden Valley Lane,
where a left-turn brings you down to the A431.

Cross the A431, and follow Church Lane down towards St Mary's
church. On reaching the war memorial, turn right to follow the
footpath out of the churchyard to reach a quiet lane. Turn right and,
in 30 yards, just past Court House, turn left onto a footpath
signposted to Keynsham. Cross the river Boyd and continue along
the track ahead for just 20 yards to a stile on the right-hand side.
Cross this stile, follow the right-hand field boundary to the next
stile, and follow the perimeter of the next field for 600 yards all the
way around to the Old Railway Line. Ignore a stone slab stile en
route on your right.

Pass beneath the railway bridge before climbing the steps on the left up the railway embankment to the old trackbed. Turn right and follow the trackbed for close on 1 mile, almost as far as a substantial bridge across the river Avon. This elevated section of the railway brings magnificent views of the hills running down to the river Avon, with Kelston Round Hill – decked with a clump of trees – being a particular landmark. Twenty yards before the bridge, descend some steps on the right to reach the Avon. Follow the riverside path beneath the Old Railway, and across four fields back towards Swineford ... those shallows where Bladud drove his pigs have long since disappeared now that the river is fully navigable! In the final field, the path leaves the river to follow a tributary stream back across the field to the A431 and the clearly visible Swan Inn.

# **Stanton Drew**
## The Druids Arms

## 15

The quiet village of Stanton Drew deep in the Chew Valley is best known for its archaeological relics – a stone circle and a cove. These ancient relics are probably Neolithic, dating from some time between 2000 and 1400 BC. This history lesson is not entirely unconnected with the village pub. The Druids Arms is so named because it was once believed that the stone circles were connected with the ancient Celtic priesthood. In reality, the Druids did not appear until many centuries after the stones were erected. This historical inaccuracy can be largely blamed upon the fertile imagination of William Stukeley, the 18th-century antiquarian.

The Druids Arms is in fact part of a terrace of cottages that front onto the main street through the village. Constructed of local stone, with hanging baskets and picnic tables either side of the front porch, this friendly local presents a pleasant exterior to its customers. Inside are the public and lounge bars, a mix of natural stone, plaster and occasional beams. With its low ceilings, open fireplaces, cushioned bench and wall seats and brasses, the Druids Arms has a very traditional feel. Around the walls are a number of rural prints and local pictures. These feature the thatched tollhouse on the edge of the village, the various local archaeological relics and the inn itself.

A good range of bar food is available at the inn including ploughman's lunches, jacket potatoes, rolls, sandwiches and toasted sandwiches. There are also more substantial offerings for larger appetites including starters such as jacket wedges and garlic bread, and main courses which include pork chops, lasagne, broccoli and cream cheese bake, tuna pasta bake and steak and kidney pie. If you can manage a third course, ice cream or lemon sorbet would make an ideal light dessert.

Traditionalists will enjoy the home-made specials available on the menu. These include such classic English dishes as hotpot, liver and onions and faggots and mushy peas!

On warm summer days, your pint can be enjoyed in the pleasant rear garden at the Druids Arms. This might be a glass of Ruddles or Wadworth 6X or Courage Best Bitter. The garden is also the site of the cove, a setting of three substantial standing stones.

Telephone: 01275 332230.

*Stanton Drew Court.*

*How to get there:* Follow the B3130 eastwards from Chew Magna towards the A37 and Pensford for just over 1 mile, before turning off onto an unclassified road signposted to Stanton Drew. This junction is marked by a rather attractive thatched tollhouse. Drive through the village, and you will find the Druids Arms on the southern edge of Stanton Drew.

*Parking:* There is a large car park for patrons beside the Druids Arms, as well as room for careful roadside parking in the vicinity of the inn.

*Length of the walk:* 3 miles. Map: OS Landranger 172 Bristol and Bath (inn GR 597631).

*Although Stanton Drew is essentially a collection of solid 18th and 19th-century houses, the history of the village goes back to Neolithic times when three stone circles were erected beside the river Chew. The 27 stones stand in a field adjacent to Church Farm, the largest circle being some 350 ft in diameter. From the village, our steps climb to the neighbouring hilltop settlement of Norton Malreward, itself overlooked by the hill and Iron Age earthworks of Maes Knoll. As a complete contrast to all this austere prehistory, the walk follows a short section of the river Chew back towards Stanton Drew, a calm and placid backwater!*

## The Walk

Turn right outside the Druids Arms and follow the road northwards out of Stanton Drew, over the Chew and onto the junction with the B3130. A magnificent thatched tollhouse stands at this junction. Turn right and pass the nearby garage before turning left onto an unsignposted minor road. Follow this quiet lane through open countryside for just over 1 mile to the village of Norton Malreward. The lane climbs uphill into the village where, just past a telephone box, you turn right along a drive leading to the church.

Just before the first set of gates giving access to the church, turn right onto a track which is followed around the eastern boundary of the churchyard. Immediately past the end of the churchyard, the track bears right and heads across an open hilltop field for ½ mile. It is worth pausing to enjoy the views back to Maes Knoll and southwards across the Chew Valley. At the far side of the open

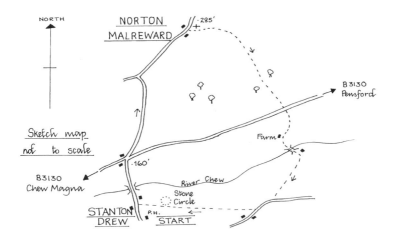

hilltop section of the walk, the path reaches a belt of trees, beyond which it follows a shady, enclosed course downhill for 300 yards to reach the B3130.

The return leg of the walk back to Stanton Drew follows well-defined and well-signposted fieldpaths, but the directions are of necessity somewhat detailed and complex. Do not worry – it is not nearly as difficult as it sounds, with marker arrows appearing on most stiles and gateposts along the way.

On reaching the B3130, turn left for just a few yards before crossing a stile on the right-hand side. Follow the field boundary parallel to the road back in a westerly direction for just 50 yards to a stile in the corner of the field. Beyond this stile, turn left and follow the field boundary downhill to a stile in the bottom corner of the field. Once across this stile, bear half-right, clipping the corner of the field, to reach another stile in the right-hand hedgerow. Continue straight across the next couple of fields, passing through gateways along the way, to reach a lane that runs alongside Byemills Farm.

Turn left, and follow the lane down to the river Chew. Cross the river by way of a stone bridge and the adjoining sluice, before crossing a stile on the right-hand side to follow a section of the

73

signposted Two Rivers Way. Follow the well-worn riverside path across the next three fields and, having passed through a gateway in the far left-hand corner of the third field, follow the right-hand field boundary in the next field onto the Pensford to Stanton Drew road.

Turn right, and follow this narrow lane for 200 yards to a gateway on the right. Pass through this gateway, bear left and follow a signposted path directly across two fields used for market gardening. You are heading in the direction of Stanton Drew church which is clearly visible on the skyline. The path bears left at the far side of the second field, following the hedgerow for 25 yards until you come to a stile in the hedgerow. Beyond this stile, cross to a gate in the far right-hand corner of the next field. It is now simply a matter of crossing the next field to join that prominent dirt track on the right that leads back into Stanton Drew. Along the way, you will pass the stone circle in a field on the right, before passing Church Farm and the village church. The track joins a lane which heads down to the main street in Stanton Drew, where a left-turn will return you to the Druids Arms.

# **Dundry**
## The Carpenters Tavern

**16**

Follow the Roman road out of South Bristol and over Dundry Hill towards the Chew Valley, and you will pass through the roadside settlement of Maiden Head, on the fringes of Dundry. There on the hilltop stands the Carpenters Tavern, a popular hostelry with visitors from Bristol enjoying a day out in the neighbouring countryside. The inn, with its whitewashed walls, black paintwork and hanging baskets, presents a handsome exterior.

Internally, there are a series of interconnected rooms, including a restaurant/carvery. All the bar areas have low ceilings, and a large number of dark beams, which contrast with the inn's white paintwork. From the ceilings hang various items of horse memorabilia, including saddles, harnesses and yokes, whilst around the walls are displayed a number of prints. On one of the windows sills, a collection of china pigs is on display! With its pew seats, wooden furniture and fine old fireplaces, the Carpenters Tavern enjoys a really traditional atmosphere.

The bar menu includes omelettes, ploughman's lunches, sandwiches, salads, filled jacket potatoes, hot pot dishes and snacks, whilst each day a number of special dishes are displayed on the board in the bar. These could include such tempting options as cream and garlic mushroom puffs, vegetable dipper, seafood bolognese, chicken stir fry, crab salad, Dover sole and savoury mince-filled pitta bread. Fish dishes are a speciality, but do carry a warning – all fish is freshly delivered, and prices are only a guide. What you will actually pay depends on the size of each fish!

To the rear of the inn is a large garden area, complete with picnic tables and children's play area. On a hot summer's day, the garden is justifiably popular with patrons enjoying a refreshing pint of beer. The brews on offer might include John Smith's Bitter, Courage Bitter and Directors, and Butcombe Bitter brewed in a nearby village of the same name.

Telephone: 01179 640415.

*How to get there:* Follow the old Roman road out of South Bristol, through Bishopsworth and Withywood, and onto Dundry Hill. A mile out of the city, just as you reach the hilltop, the Carpenters Tavern lies alongside the road in the hamlet of Maiden Head, ½ mile from Dundry village.

*Parking:* There is a large car park for patrons behind the Carpenters Tavern, as well as roadside parking beside the inn on the lane leading to Norton Hawkfield.

*Length of the walk:* 3 miles. Map: OS Landranger 172 Bristol and Bath (inn GR 565663).

*From Maiden Head, the walk follows fieldpaths and lanes through to the neighbouring village of Dundry. Dundry church is a landmark that is familiar to most Bristolians, situated high on the skyline above the city's southern suburbs. This walk provides the opportunity to enjoy the view in reverse, with the hilltop path east of Dundry overlooking one of the most famous cities in the land. It is a panorama that few Bristolians take the opportunity to enjoy. From the breezy hilltops, the walk descends into East Dundry, a delightful hillside settlement overlooking a tributary stream of the river Chew, before returning to Maiden Head.*

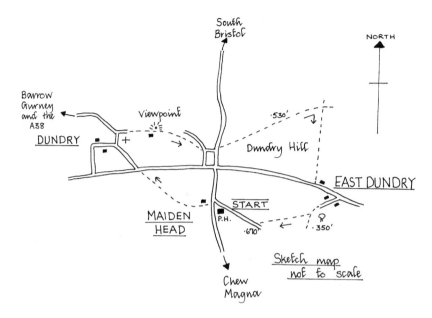

## The Walk

Across the road from the front of the Carpenters Tavern, a small lane runs beside a couple of new houses. Follow this lane to a stile, and the open fields beyond. Follow the right-hand field boundary across the first field to another stile, before bearing half-left to reach a third stile in the far corner of the next field. This stile brings you out alongside a road junction. Follow the road ahead, signposted to Dundry. This is actually Church Road, which brings you to the village church in just ¼ mile.

Immediately past the church, turn right and continue down to the bend by the village school. At this point, turn right along a cul-de-sac lane, which runs along the northern edge of the churchyard. In little more than ¼ mile, this lane ends in a small parking area, with expansive views to the north across the whole of the city of Bristol. The Clifton Suspension Bridge is but one landmark to pinpoint. Beyond this parking area, continue along the hillside, now following a footpath. The path shortly passes through a gateway alongside a farm, before continuing along the bottom edge of a field. In the far corner of this field, cross a wooden barrier and follow the path on in the same direction until you reach a secluded road junction.

Follow the lane opposite – Oxleaze Lane – for 150 yards to its junction with Broad Oak Hill. Cross the road, and continue along the bridlepath opposite. This runs as a metalled lane to a bungalow, before continuing as an unmetalled track. Half a mile on from Broad Oak Hill, this bridlepath reaches open fields. Follow the left-hand hedgerow across the next two fields, still high above the streets of Bristol, to the corner of the second field. At this point, turn right and follow the field boundary away from the edge of the hill and in the direction of the mast on the hilltop. The path crosses a couple of fields to reach a lane that runs past the mast and on to a road junction by North Hill Farm.

Follow the lane to the left, down into the East Dundry. On a bend in the village, just past Cross Cottage, turn right along Spring Lane, a cul-de-sac. This lane runs down the hillside past a number of fine cottages, before continuing as a footpath through the trees to the stream in the valley bottom. Once across the stream, the path forks. Bear right, and you will soon reach a rudimentary – but functional – stile that leads into a hillside pasture. Follow the path up the hillside to the top right-hand corner of the field, where you will find another stile. The view back across to East Dundry is worth pausing to enjoy.

Beyond this stile, follow the hedgerow on the right across the next field to a gateway/gap in the corner. In one final field, head half-left across to Watercress Farm. Aim for a gate that lies in the middle of the complex of farm buildings. Bear left along a track beyond this gate, which leads up to the lane leading back to Maiden Head. Turn right, and the Carpenters Tavern is less than $\frac{1}{2}$ mile along the road.

# East Harptree
## The Waldegrave Arms

The Waldegrave family have dominated life around Chewton Mendip and East Harptree for many years. As far back as the 16th century, the family owned the Chewton lead minery, one of four lead reeves on the Mendips. The Waldegraves were later to become involved in the coal-mining industry in North Somerset, as well as being amongst the area's great landowners. It comes as little surprise, therefore, to find such a ruling dynasty lending their name to one of the local hostelries.

Tucked away in a corner of East Harptree, forming an attractive group of buildings that include the village church and a local farmhouse, is the Waldegrave Arms. Constructed of the sturdy local stone, this off-the-beaten-track inn is deceptively spacious and roomy. In addition to the public and lounge bars, patrons can also enjoy such facilities as the restaurant, the stable bar, the games room, courtyard seating and a pleasant back lawn.

The Waldegrave Arms exudes a real sense of history, with its stone fireplaces, beams and oak tables. Around the inn are displayed various brass and copper artefacts, as well as prints,

79

photographs and maps. Whether you choose to relax in the traditional bar areas, or to enjoy the Mendip air in the gardens, you can be sure of a meal that is both well presented and good value for money. The bar menu includes starters, jacket potatoes, snacks, chicken dishes, fish dishes, ploughman's lunches, rolls and steaks, with a range of specials being chalked up in the bar each day. These might include chicken soup, roast beef, roast pork, chicken curry or cream cheese and broccoli bake.

The Waldegrave Arms is now owned by Ushers, the Trowbridge-based brewery. One of their fine beers should be almost obligatory following a stroll across the hilly Mendip countryside – perhaps a pint of Best, Founders or Triple Crown. A delightful walk followed by an excellent pint in one of the area's finest old pubs – all the ingredients for a perfect day out!

Telephone: 01761 221429.

*How to get there:* Leave the A368 Bath to Weston-super-Mare road at West Harptree, and follow the B3114 Chewton Mendip turning. In less than 1 mile, turn off onto the unclassified road leading into

*Relics of the lead mining industry in the Mendips.*

East Harptree village. At the top of this road, at the junction by the village shop, turn right. The Waldegrave Arms lies 100 yards along the road on the left-hand side, opposite the village church.

*Parking:* There is a car park for patrons alongside the Waldegrave Arms, as well as roadside parking in the vicinity of the inn.

*Length of the walk:* 3 miles. Map: OS Landranger 182 Weston-super-Mare and Bridgwater (inn GR 565560).

*Tucked away in a secluded corner of the Mendip Hills, this delightful walk is full of the most unexpected surprises. Other than the magnificent natural landscape of rolling hills and far-ranging views, you will be surprised to discover relics of Mendip's lead mining industry tucked away in secluded woodland, as well as a spectacular water-board aqueduct hidden deep in Harptree Combe. The combe itself is a very special place in springtime, with its rippling brook and extensive range of flora. There is a climb of 450 ft between the Waldegrave Arms and the remains of the lead industry in East Harptree Wood, but every bead of perspiration is well rewarded!*

## The Walk

From the Waldegrave Arms, walk along Church Lane, past the Village Stores and out of East Harptree. Some 150 yards past Water Street, turn right onto a signposted footpath. Follow this path across three fields, keeping to the right-hand edge of each field, until you reach Highfield Lane. Turn left for a few yards, before turning right into a cul-de-sac lane shown on the OS sheet as Morgan's Lane.

Follow this lane uphill for 400 yards until you reach signposted footpaths on the right-hand side. Cross the stile at this point, and follow the footpath directly ahead that runs alongside the right-hand field boundary. The views at this point extend to Chew Valley Lake. In 150 yards, pass through a gate on the right into the adjoining field and descend to its far left-hand corner. At this point, a stile alongside a stream brings you out onto Wallace Lane.

Turn left, and follow this lane for 300 yards to its junction with Smitham Hill, alongside Mead Cottage. Turn left, and climb the hill for almost ½ mile until you reach Sycamore Cottage on the right-hand side. Immediately past this cottage, turn right along a track. In

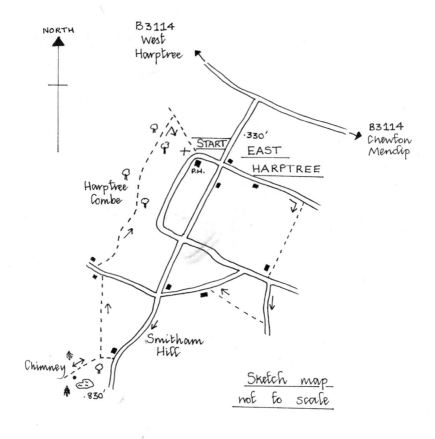

50 yards, where the track bears right, cross the stile directly ahead into an open field. Follow the right-hand field boundary to a stile at the far side of this field, before continuing through East Harptree Wood to the chimney of the former lead smelting works and its neighbouring pond. Do not let words like lead and smelter put you off – this is now a delightful rural idyll!

Retrace your steps back through the woods and across the field to the rear of Sycamore Cottage. Do not return to the lane, but rather bear left along the track behind Sycamore Cottage to reach a gateway. Cross the field beyond this gate to a stile in the opposite hedgerow, from where extensive views can be enjoyed across the Chew Valley. In the next field, descend to a pair of stiles in the bottom right-hand corner. Once across the second of these stiles,

*Aqueduct deep in Harptree Combe.*

bear sharp left down the side of the next field to reach a gate at the foot of the slope which gives access to Western Lane.

Turn left and, in just 100 yards, turn right across a stile. Two footpaths are signposted – follow the right-hand footpath across an area of scrubland to a stile and the entrance to Harptree Combe. Follow the stream northwards down through the combe. In ½ mile, the humps and mounds bordering a clearing are all that remain of the ancient Richmond Castle. Continue beyond this clearing, bearing left at the foot of a flight of steps to follow the path as it passes beneath an aqueduct carrying a water pipeline. About 250 yards beyond this aqueduct, the path leaves the combe to enter an open field. Turn sharp right up the slope, and follow a path across three fields to reach East Harptree church. A squeeze-belly stile leads to a path alongside the church, which is followed down to the Waldegrave Arms.

# 18 **Blagdon**
## The Live and Let Live

The village of Blagdon lies on the lower slopes of the Mendip Hills, its slight elevation bringing extensive views across the nearby Chew Valley. Although lying on a busy thoroughfare from Bath to Weston, the handsome properties along the village's quiet side roads prove ever popular with commuters to nearby Bristol. Back on the main road we find one of the village's three inns, the Live and Let Live. With its freshly-painted exterior, timber, plasterwork and adjoining beer garden, the inn offers a pleasing prospect to both locals and passing motorists.

Internally, the Live and Let Live consists of a lounge bar, a games room and a restaurant. The lounge has a very traditional feel, with inglenook fireplace, beams and darkwood tables and chairs and cushioned seats. Around the lounge are displayed brasses, prints of rural scenes, various copper artefacts and even an old rifle! Walkers will undoubtedly be attracted by a pair of detailed maps of the nearby reservoirs – Blagdon Lake and Chew Valley Lake.

A range of traditional bar food is available at the Live and Let Live. Snacks include home-made soup, filled jacket potatoes, large filled rolls and well-presented open prawn sandwiches. More substantial dishes are also available including cottage pie, chicken Kiev and vegetable chilli. Children are catered for with their own range of dishes, whilst in the adjoining restaurant a full selection of excellent food is available. With the landlord being a trout fisherman, it comes as no surprise to find trout on the menu!

The Live and Let Live is owned by Ushers, the Trowbridge-based brewery. The famous West Country brewery was founded as long ago as 1824, but lost its independence when taken over by Watney in 1960. Following a management buyout in 1991, it has invested heavily in pubs and plant in order to re-establish its reputation for excellence. Amongst its fine beers you might care to sample with your meal are Ushers Best Bitter, Founders Ale and its Special brew.

Telephone: 01761 462403.

*How to get there:* Blagdon lies on the A368 Bath to Weston-super-Mare road, just 4 miles east of the junction with the A38 at Churchill. The Live and Let Live is located on the eastern edge of the village, fronting onto the main road.

*Blagdon lake.*

*Parking:* There is a car park for patrons to the rear of the Live and Let Live. There is also room for roadside parking in Score Lane, the quiet side road that runs beside the inn.

*Length of the walk:* 4½ miles. Map: OS Landranger 172 Bristol and Bath (inn GR 504587).

*Blagdon and Ubley are two attractive commuter-villages 10 miles south of Bristol, just above the shoreline of Blagdon Lake, one of Bristol's major reservoirs, and tucked beneath the northern slopes of the Mendip Hills. This walk begins with a stiff climb out of Blagdon onto the Mendip hilltops, where a section of level upland walking brings far-reaching views across the local countryside. The path descends steeply into Ubley, where level fieldpaths are followed back into Blagdon. This last section of the walk brings extensive views towards Blagdon Lake, lying just ¼ mile to the north.*

## The Walk

Alongside the Live and Let Live runs Score Lane. Follow this quiet cul-de-sac lane uphill and, where the tarmac ends, continue along a short section of enclosed path to a stile. Beyond this stile, head uphill towards the top left-hand corner of the field to another stile, before continuing along a track to Leaze Farm. Pass to the right of the farm buildings, cross the farm access road and continue on uphill along Leaze Lane, a green track. In 50 yards, Leaze Lane bears to the left and heads across the Mendip hilltops, well over 400 ft above the Live and Let Live! The views to the north across both Blagdon and Chew Lakes are quite superb.

In just ½ mile, the enclosed section of Leaze Lane ends at a gateway. Follow the left-hand field boundary of the next field to a stile in the far left-hand corner, beyond which you reach a track called Ubley Drove. Turn left and follow Ubley Drove downhill, eventually passing through Ubley Wood and onto a lane on the edge of a hamlet called Ubley Sideling. One hundred yards down this lane, cross a stone slab stile on the left in front of Lake View Cottage. Follow the signposted path downhill to a gateway and the A368.

Turn left for just a few yards, before following a footpath on the opposite side of the road beyond an iron stile down into Ubley. This path follows the right-hand edge of a field before continuing as

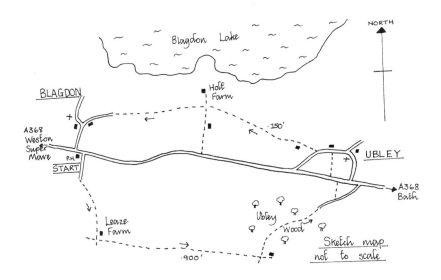

an enclosed path down to The Street and Ubley school. Turn left along The Street for 200 yards. Where it bears to the left, continue ahead along Frog Lane, a cul-de-sac. In 200 yards the lane ends at Ubley Farm. Keep to the right of the farm buildings and continue into an open field.

The return to Blagdon follows fieldpaths for 1½ miles. The directions of necessity are rather detailed, but rest assured that things are not quite so complicated on the ground! Follow the track ahead across to a gateway on the right of this field, beyond which the right-of-way bears sharply to the left to head across to a gate/stile in the opposite hedgerow. In the next field, cross to a stile in the far right-hand corner, enjoying all the while views to the north of Blagdon Lake and to the south of the Mendip escarpment. Cross the next field to a clearly visible stile in the opposite hedgerow, before crossing a much larger field to reach a gate/stile which brings you out behind some factory premises.

Cross a driveway that leads down to Holt Farm, using clearly visible stiles either side of the lane, before passing through a small area of woodland to reach an open field. Blagdon village, especially its prominent church, can be seen ¾ mile ahead. Head in the direction of Blagdon, following a gravelled track beside the right-hand field boundary. One hundred yards beyond a small fishing pond, pass through a gateway and continue along the opposite side of the hedgerow to a stile in the corner of the field. Cross this stile, and continue along the edge of the next field for just 100 yards before crossing another stile on your left to reach an enclosed pathway.

Follow this enclosed track into Blagdon, where it becomes a metalled lane. Turn left at the junction of this lane with Church Street, and continue uphill to the A368. Across the road, you will find the Live and Let Live and what will be a welcoming pint after this strenuous excursion on the Mendip Hills.

*The village of Ubley.*

# Churchill
**19**
## The Crown Inn

Passing motorists are probably glad to see the back of Churchill, as they escape the queues at the junction of the A38 with the A368 Bath to Weston road. The Crown lies at the top of Skinners Lane, a quiet byway well away from Churchill's main thoroughfares. Constructed of the local stone, this former cottage has earned a reputation for being one of the most unspoilt pubs in the area. With its stone and slate floors, beams, stone fireplaces, wall benches and settles, it is not difficult to see why the inn has proved particularly popular with customers seeking a traditional pub atmosphere.

The name of the village has nothing to do with Winston – it simply translates literally to 'the church on the hill'. In the 17th and 18th centuries, the village grew up as a mining settlement, with local men extracting calamine from beneath the Mendips for use in Bristol's brass foundries. Miners have always had a reputation for strong thirsts, and those miners from centuries past would surely find the Crown a pub to their liking.

The Crown offers a good range of food to its customers, including home-made soup, ploughman's lunches, salads and sandwiches.

More substantial appetites wil be tempted by perhaps the steak and kidney pie, chilli or rabbit casserole. It is the wide selection of beers that has earned the Crown its real popularity, however. There can be as many as a dozen real ales available at the bar! These might typically include Butcombe Bitter, Old Speckled Hen, Palmers IPA and Eldridge Pope's Thomas Hardy Bitter. There is even a house beer, Batch Bitter, brewed by the Cotleigh Brewery of Wiveliscombe. The Crown also offers its customers a fine selection of country wines, including one particular wine from nearby Axbridge.

Whatever the season of the year, you will undoubtedly enjoy a visit to the Crown at the end of a walk on the Mendip Hills. In midwinter, the roaring log fires will soon put the warmth back into your system, whilst in high summer your refreshing pint can be enjoyed in the inn's rear garden.

Telephone: 01934 852995.

*How to get there:* Follow the A368 Weston road from the traffic lights in the centre of Churchill for 200 yards, until you reach the Nelson's Arms pub on the left-hand side. Turn left by this pub into Skinners Lane, at the top of which you will find what appears to be an isolated cottage. This is the Crown.

*Parking:* The Batch, a wide unmetalled byway in front of the Crown, offers parking space for a fair number of vehicles.

*Length of the walk:* 3 miles. Map: OS Landranger 172 Bristol and Bath (inn GR 445596).

*A walk of great contrasts. The outward leg of this excursion follows Dolebury Bottom, a deep wooded valley nestling at the southern slopes of Dolebury Hill. The return journey back to Churchill sees the walk crossing the high, open slopes of Dolebury itself, the location of the finest hillfort on the Mendips. The views are quite exceptional, and encompass much of West Mendip, the Chew Valley, the Bristol Channel and the distant Welsh Hills. Given the Mendips' fearsome reputation for poor weather, wait until a ridge of high pressure is firmly in place before attempting this walk!*

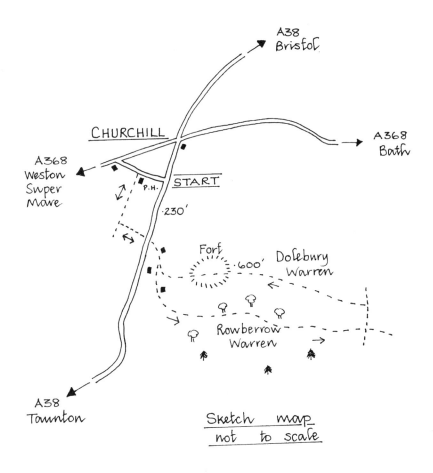

A38
Bristol

A368
Bath

CHURCHILL

A368
Weston
Super
Mare

P.H.

START

·230'

Fort
·600'   Dolebury
Warren

Rowberrow
Warren

A38
Taunton

Sketch   map
not   to   scale

## The Walk

Follow the Batch, the unmetalled lane in front of the Crown, uphill for 200 yards. Opposite Dinghurst Cottage, turn left along a bridlepath which leads downhill through the trees to the busy A38. Cross the main road with care, and follow the lane opposite – Doleberrow. This is an access drive to a number of secluded properties, as well as a public right-of-way. The drive climbs for 200 yards, before descending to join a lane alongside a cottage called The Oak House. Turn left along this lane, which becomes an unmetalled bridlepath in just 150 yards.

Follow this bridlepath beyond a parking area and gate for the next 1¼ miles. It runs along a wooded valley bottom, in the shadow of the steep southern slopes of Dolebury Hill. Ignore a couple of prominent right turns along the way, continuing on to a cross track a little way beyond a Forestry Commission sign on the right – Rowberrow Warren.

Turn left at the cross track and, in just 50 yards, left again at a gateway onto the path that leads to Dolebury Hillfort. A National Trust information board by the gate gives extensive details of this feature. To reach the hillfort, head straight across the first open field to a gate/stile in the far corner. Continue along the right-hand edge of the next field, hawthorn bushes on the right, for just 100 yards until you reach a marker post on the right signposted 'The Limestone Link'. Turn right at this point, following a path through the bushes. This path soon bears to the left, around the edge of a coniferous plantation, before continuing westwards across sheep-cropped turf to a gate/stile. Beyond this stile, continue uphill to the hilltop and the hillfort site. The views are exceptional, giving a magnificent panorama of West Mendip.

Pass through the middle of the hillfort, and descend the slopes of the hilltop to a gap in the western rampart. The path bears left, then right, down through the woodland to a gateway deep in Dolebury Bottom. Beyond this gate, you will soon rejoin that access drive – Doleberrow – walked earlier. Follow this drive to the right back to the A38, cross to the bridlepath opposite and climb through the trees back to the Batch. A right turn will soon find you back at the Crown.

# 20 Clevedon
## The Little Harp Inn

Clevedon is a somewhat genteel seaside resort, sitting proudly above its pebbly foreshore on the Bristol Channel. The Victorian air that pervades the town is best seen in the large grey limestone villas that line the streets leading to the seafront. Built of the same austere stone is the Little Harp, a solid public house that stands beside the resort's promenade overlooking the Channel.

The Little Harp, the subject of extensive refurbishment in recent years, is spread over three levels. Families are welcome in both the upstairs and basement areas. The inn is comfortably furnished with carpets throughout, reproduction furniture sets and cushioned settles. Timbered ceilings and attractive lamps complete the decor, whilst plates, brasses and prints add a homely touch to the inn. Perhaps the most popular part of the Little Harp is the conservatory with fine views across the Bristol Channel ... although on hot sunny days patrons may prefer the picnic tables out in the garden.

An extensive menu awaits visitors to the Little Harp. The selections cover starters, children's dishes, lighter bites, specials, salads, fish dishes, grills, meat and poultry, baked potatoes, sandwiches, ploughman's lunches and desserts. The specials featured on a recent visit included meatloaf, oriental spare ribs and sausage plait, whilst the fish menu included grilled wild Pacific salmon with peppered prawn nests. With desserts such as banana and fudge shuffle and raspberry rapture, you can be assured that the heartiest of appetites will soon be satisfied at the Little Harp.

The inn is a freehouse, and offers a good selection of beers and ales. These might include the somewhat ubiquitous John Smith's Bitter, or Marston's Pedigree or Bitter. Either way, following a gentle stroll along Clevedon's relaxing foreshore, you will find a hospitable welcome at this busy seafront hostelry.

Telephone: 01275 343739.

*How to get there:* Leave junction 20 on the M5 motorway and follow the signs to Clevedon's seafront. Within 200 yards of a sharp right turn that sees the road heading along parallel to the foreshore, separated from it by a large grassed play area, you will find the Little Harp on the left-hand side.

*Parking:* There is a car park for patrons beside the Little Harp, as well as roadside parking immediately outside the inn.

*Length of the walk:* 2 miles. Map: OS Landranger 172 Bristol and Bath (inn GR 399714).

*Clevedon is a traditional Victorian resort on the Bristol Channel coast, best known for the iron pier that inspired the poet John Betjeman: 'It recalls a painting by Turner, or an etching by Whistler or Sickert, or even a Japanese print. Without its pier, Clevedon would be a diamond with a flaw.'*

*This short walk explores the south-western end of the promenade before climbing onto Church Hill and Wain's Hill, an upland area that forms a headland with extensive views across the Channel towards the Welsh coast. The walk around the headland has been designated as the Poet's Walk by the local council, on account of its popularity with the poet Coleridge when he resided in nearby Old Church Road. The quite magnificent view of the town's esplanade and its pier obtained on the return leg of the walk is certain to inspire even the most unpoetic into verse!*

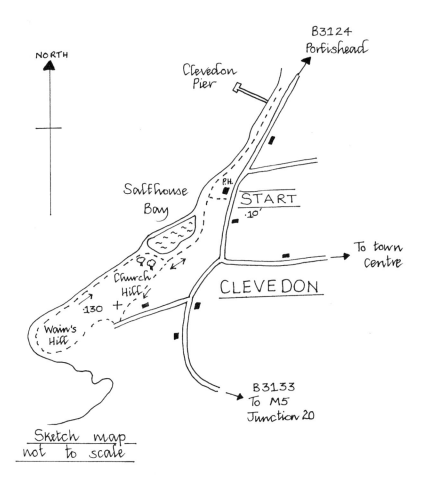

NORTH

B3124
Portishead

Clevedon
Pier

Saulthouse
Bay

P.H.

START
·10'

To town
Centre

Church
Hill

CLEVEDON

·130 +

Wain's
Hill

B3133
To M5
Junction 20

Sketch map
not to scale

## The Walk

From the Little Harp, walk to the promenade and head off in a south-westerly direction (ie to the left!). At the far end of the prom, climb the steps into the woodland that clings to the slopes of Church Hill. At the entrance to the woods, you will find a detailed information board explaining why this part of the town has been designated as the Poet's Walk. Ignore any side turns, and simply climb the steps to the top of the hillside, where you leave the tree cover behind to enjoy the first of many extensive views on this walk.

Cross to the far side of Church Hill, where a path on the left leads down to a tarmac path. Follow this path to the right until it emerges by St Andrew's church. Continue along the drive ahead, beside the cemetery, down to Old Church Road. Turn right, and in 200 yards you will find yourself by a gateway with a small boatyard complex immediately ahead.

Just past this gateway, turn right onto the main path that begins to climb onto Wain's Hill – there is another Poet's Walk information board. Follow this path up to the south-western tip of the headland, where a conveniently placed seat will enable you to enjoy fine Channel views both down to Weston-super-Mare and across to the Welsh coast.

From the tip of the headland, continue following the tarmac path around the coast and back towards Clevedon. The path passes beside the churchyard, beyond which fine views of Clevedon's seafront and the noted Victorian pier open up. Keep on the path all the way back to the old boating lake, where the path bears to the right to rejoin the promenade. It is now a simple matter of retracing your steps to the Little Harp.

*Clevedon church.*